# A Guide to the Internet for Churches & Pastors

by
Steven M.
Murray

**DISCIPLESHIP** RESOURCES

P.O. BOX 840 • NASHVILLE, TENNESSEE 37202-0840

www.disciplineshipresources.org

Cover and book design by Sharon Anderson

ISBN 0-88177-244-5

Library of Congress Card Catalog No. 98-70292

DR244

I would like to extend my thanks to a number of people who helped make this book possible:

- Henk Pieterse and the staff of the publishing team and of Discipleship Resources, who encouraged me to undertake this project and who offered valuable insight throughout;

- Phil, our "webmaster," who got me online, and the rest of the community at St. Matthews United Methodist Church, who have put up with me for all these years;

- Bill and Anne Marie, my brother and sister-in-law, who taught me much of what I know about the Internet;

- my mom and Walt, who are constant reminders that learning is a lifelong process;

- my wife, Nicole, and my sons, Christopher and Samuel, who lovingly support me and who gave up family time so I could work on this book;

- most of all, to my Lord and Savior Jesus Christ, who gives meaning and purpose to all.

Thank you all!

Steven M. Murray
St. Matthews United Methodist Church
Sandown, New Hampshire


"For I am not ashamed of the gospel..."
Romans 1:16

In 1455 Johann Gutenberg produced the first printed Bible. Suddenly an item once available only to the privileged few was now widely accessible. No longer was it necessary for monks to painstakingly copy the Scriptures by hand. No longer were the common people denied the gospel. Today the Bible, once so costly to produce, is printed so inexpensively that we can give it away on street corners. The advent of the printing press revolutionized our world. It allowed not only the Bible but also a seemingly infinite collection of printed information to become available to the masses.

It's no exaggeration to say that the advent of the Internet represents a similar information revolution. Perhaps the one significant difference between the printed word and the Internet is the accessibility of information. When relying on the printed word, the reader is limited to the books available to him or her. Most of us have a collection of personal books; many of us are fortunate enough to live within reasonable distance of a public library. But even the information available in a large city library pales in comparison to that available through the Internet. Information on the Internet is available in equal measure to people in every remote corner of the earth.

The Internet is a powerful information tool that represents a revolution in communication. Through the wonders of e-mail, chat rooms, and newsgroups, users can communicate across town or across the world with the same speed, cost, and ease. Through e-mail attachments and file transfers, documents and other information can be shared quickly and easily.

Before going too much further, let me say a few words about terminology. The church has a language of its own. We speak of *atonement, conversion, justification,* and *sanctification.* To refer to ourselves, we use acronyms such as UMC for United

Methodist Church; ELCA for Evangelical Lutheran Church of America; and UCC for United Church of Christ. In the UMC we're especially fond of using acronyms for the names of our ministries. After all, everyone knows what the UMYF, UMW, and PPR are, right? But many who are new to the church find the buzzwords, the theological terms, and the acronyms as unintelligible as a foreign language. For newcomers, "church talk" can be confusing and intimidating.

It's no different with the Internet. It also has a language all its own—one that's packed with technical terms, acronyms, abbreviations, and trendy buzzwords. Not surprisingly, newcomers to the Internet often find it confusing, frustrating, and even intimidating.

To help you become comfortable with the language of the Internet, key terms and phrases are defined in the margins on the pages with the words.

There's no question that the Internet is making a significant impact on North American society. One can hardly turn on the television or read a newspaper without noticing references to web sites and e-mail addresses. At any social gathering, you're almost certain to find at least a few people swapping stories of their latest discoveries in cyberspace. The real issue becomes: Where does the church fit in, if at all?

Throughout the book we will address the question of how the church may relate to the Internet. We also will talk about some of the common concerns that church members have. My hope is to make the Internet understandable and accessible to the layperson and to the pastor. Once they're on the Internet, many Christians and churches have found it to be a valuable tool for personal enrichment and for ministry. I believe you will too.

Steven M. Murray

# *Making Sense of the Internet:*

# A Few FAQs

If you're like many people in our society, you have heard just enough about the Internet to have a lot of questions, but few answers. Unfortunately, this condition often leads to partial understanding or even misconception. I've met Christians who are fearful of, or even vehemently opposed to, the "Net" (an abbreviation for Internet). Most often, these people have never used the Internet and know little about what it is or how it works.

In this chapter we will try to answer many of the **FAQs** you may have about the Internet, such as the following: Where did the Internet come from? Who controls it? What does it cost to get **online**? What kind of computer do I need to buy? What's allowed on the Net? Once some of these basic questions have been addressed, we will be in a position to face the real question: How can I as a Christian, and my church, benefit from the Internet?

**FAQs:**
Frequently Asked Questions. A set of commonly asked questions, with answers, posted to keep people from having to ask the same things repeatedly. Newsgroups and many web pages include a FAQ section.

**ONLINE:**
Term for being connected to the Internet.

7

## A BIT OF HISTORY

Where did the Internet come from? The Internet traces its history back to a government project in the late 1960's. Even though computers in those early years were slow and cumbersome, many people already could see potential. Once mainframe computers began appearing in universities, government offices, and some businesses, researchers turned their attention to connecting them over large distances. The U.S. Department of Defense's Advanced Research Projects Agency (ARPA) first took up this challenge in earnest. Building such a network would require the development of both new technology and common standards so that the computers could interrelate. In essence, they needed the hardware to connect the computers and a new common language that all the computers could speak.

In the late 1960's the Cold War and the threat of nuclear attack were primary concerns. Because of this, ARPA designed a system that didn't rely on a single central computer; instead, the system consisted of several linked computers. The system worked like this: Information was assigned a destination address and then was passed from computer to computer until it arrived at its destination. In this way, if one computer was "down" (because of nuclear attack or another catastrophic failure), the information could be rerouted to another path.

In many ways the advantages of ARPA's multiple-computer system could be compared to taking a trip by car, instead of a trip by airplane. Rather than trying to provide direct service to and from every city in the United States, many airlines have established a central terminal in one city (a hub). With the exception of a few heavily traveled routes, all passengers fly into this hub and change to planes that will take them to their destination.

On the other hand, our nation's system of roads and highways looks more like a web that connects a seemingly infinite number of cities and towns. In a cross-country road trip, thousands of potential paths to a particular destination exist.

The system used by the airlines is efficient and cost-effective. However, efficiency wasn't ARPA's primary concern. ARPA wanted tenacity! It wanted to know that information would reach its destination—even if key locations were destroyed. Cross-country air travel is dependent on any number of variables. For example, if a particular hub city is snowed in, airlines relying on that city face delays and cancellations. On the road, however, you have the option of driving around the trouble spots. It may not be the most efficient way, but it gets you there.

ARPA's computer system became known as the Advanced Research Projects Agency Network (ARPANET). In its first decade, the system was used primarily by government researchers to share information and data. However, the Department of Defense began to use this network extensively, with a focus on military application. Because of this dual application, ARPANET was split into two networks: ARPANET continued to be used for academic needs, and MILNET concentrated on the needs of the military. Although the networks were separate, information still could be shared between them.

The interconnection came to be known as the DARPA (Defense Advanced Research Projects Agency) Internet. The title was later shortened to the Internet.

Recognizing the obvious potential of such a network, the National Science Foundation provided funding for a high-speed **backbone** network in the 1980's. Returning to our roadway analogy, the effect of the backbone network was similar to that of the construction of the interstate highway system: It allowed people to travel at higher speeds with fewer forced stops. At the same time it offered a variety of highways from which to choose. If there was

**BACKBONE:**
The high-speed lines to which a network of computers is connected.

**ISP:**
Internet Service Provider. A company that, for a fee, provides a computer user with a telephone number to access the Internet. Some of the larger ISPs are *America Online*, *CompuServe*, and *Prodigy*.

"construction" on one highway, drivers could seek an alternate route.

This new networking system was known as the NSFNET (National Science Foundation Network), and by 1990 it eventually led to the dismantling of the ARPANET.

Until that point, the Internet had been limited to nonprofit usage. However, it soon became apparent that the commercial potential for such a network was tremendous. In the early 1990's a new backbone was developed for commercial use. The Commercial Internet Exchange became the conduit for commercial use of the Internet, while the NSFNET continued to support research and other nonprofit use. Once commercial use began to take place, the Internet expanded rapidly. Because of the expansion beyond its original research and government purposes, the National Science Foundation eventually withdrew its funding, leaving us with the current system that's supported entirely by commercial use.

### WHO CONTROLS THE INTERNET?

A common misconception about the Internet is that someone owns it or controls it. One logical but erroneous assumption is that the government still controls the Internet. As mentioned earlier, the U.S. government initiated the Internet; but over the past thirty years, the Internet has evolved into an entirely commercial network.

Depending on your point of view, you could say the Internet is owned by no one or by everyone. Its contents and infrastructure are provided by every user, **ISP**, school, business, or organization that uses it.

Of course, the Internet could not function without its common "language" or standards. For those standards to evolve, and yet remain consistent, there is the **InterNIC**. Along with maintaining common standards that allow millions of computers to communicate in a logical way, the InterNIC maintains the system of addresses known as the **domain name** system. Even though the InterNIC doesn't own or control the contents of the Internet, it does allow improvements and technological advancements to be introduced to the system.

### WHAT'S ALLOWED ON THE INTERNET?

The Internet has virtually no constraints on its contents. It's the ultimate expression of global free speech. This is at once a blessing and a curse. It means that you and I can speak as freely and as openly about Christ as we wish. It also means that everyone else has the same freedom, including people who traffic in material that's morally offensive. With the introduction of the **World Wide Web (WWW)**, the Internet also has become a medium for high-resolution graphics, video, and sound files. This means that we can view not only text but also sights and sounds from across the world. We can enjoy great works of art, or we can be exposed to pornography.

Does this mean that Christians should have nothing to do with the Internet? **IMHO**, no. Christ didn't call us to hide behind the walls of our church buildings; instead, he calls us to share the gospel in the world through word and deed. Christians have both a right and a responsibility to be a godly influence on this new medium, the Internet. Like every other tool of communication, the Internet can be used for good or for ill. If we were to adopt a "cocoon" mentality and withdraw from the world, there would be no Christian radio, television, magazines, or other media.

Some effort has been made to control the Internet through legislation. One problem with that is that the Internet is a global community,

**INTERNIC:**
The Internet Network Information Center. InterNIC is an organization that maintains addresses for every computer on the Internet, using the domain name system.

**DOMAIN NAME:**
The base level name used to identify and look up a particular place on the Internet. It essentially identifies an "address" on a computer. The InterNIC assigns these domain names to ensure that no two computers share the same address.

**WORLD WIDE WEB:**
A system for accessing Internet resources. The WWW, or "Web," consists of thousands of computers that allow text, graphics, sound, and video to be transmitted in a cohesive format around the world.

**IMHO:**
In My Humble Opinion. One of the abbreviations used primarily in chat rooms to speed up typed communication.

**WEB SITE:**
A web site is one or more documents (web pages) that a user can access through the World Wide Web.

**SURFING:**
A term referring to the practice of viewing web sites in search of something of interest or need.

making it virtually impossible to enforce such legislation. The greater problem, however, is that the legislation that limits pornography today easily could restrain Christian witness tomorrow.

As Christians we should deal with the sinful aspects of the Internet in the same way we deal with such influences in print or on television. We have the options to tune into a particular radio station or to buy a certain magazine. We likewise have the option of visiting or avoiding **web sites** that we find objectionable—it's our choice.

The real issue becomes how to protect our children. As Christian parents we have a responsibility to monitor what our children access on the Internet in the same way that we monitor what they watch on television and what they read. I have an eleven-year-old son who **surfs** the Internet almost daily. I've been very clear with him about what's acceptable to view and what's not. My wife and I also look over his shoulder on a regular basis— lest he be tempted to go beyond our rules. There are times when we're unable to supervise our children, but there is help for such situations. Software such as *SurfWatch* and *Cyber Sitter* allow you to limit access to web sites containing pornography, adult language, and so forth. These programs limit your child's access to the Internet based on your preferences in the same way that a. computer chip now allows parents to control what television programs their children watch.

### WHAT DO I NEED TO GET ON THE INTERNET?

To get on the Internet, you essentially need three things:
1. a computer with a modem,
2. access to a telephone line (or equivalent),
3. an Internet Service Provider or commercial online service.

## WHAT COMPUTER HARDWARE DO I NEED?

If you're relatively new to the world of home computing, there are few things more confusing than computer hardware terminology. Let's look at some key terms.

**Processor Speed**. The microprocessor is the heart of the computer. There are two variables when comparing processors: *generation* and *speed*. The generation represents a step of technological advancement. The speed, measured in megahertz (MHz), represents the rate at which information is processed within a particular generation of computers. Without going back too far, you will find the following generations within IBM-compatible personal computers (PCs): the 286, the 386, the 486, and now the Pentium and the Pentium II (or the 586 and the 686 among **Intel clones**). In the world of Apple's Macintosh, there have been similar improvements leading up to the current PowerPC chip.

Technology seems to be advancing at a rate of approximately one new generation of computers every eighteen to twenty-four months. This means that by the time this book gets into your hands, a new generation of computers most likely has already appeared! In terms of speed, the Pentium processors are astonishingly fast—and getting faster.

Still you ask: How much of this hardware do I really need to get online? You probably need a bare minimum of a 386 generation computer running at a speed of at least 16 MHz. However, you would find surfing the Internet much easier and much more enjoyable with a Pentium 166 or better. The faster the processor chip, the faster your **download** time. I began surfing the Internet using a 386. Trust me when I tell you that a 386 is painfully slow!

**Hard Drive.** The hard drive is your computer's storage space. Like closet space in your home, you can never have too much space. This

**INTEL CLONE:**
Pentium is the registered trademark of the processor manufactured by the Intel Corporation. It is used in about 90 percent of the PCs currently on the market. Cyrix and others manufacture a roughly comparable chip, but cannot use the name "Pentium."

**DOWNLOAD:**
Transferring information from another computer into your own. The opposite of download is upload, where you send information to another computer. An example of downloading is receiving e-mail. An example of uploading is posting your newly designed web page.

**GIG:**
Abbreviation of gigabyte. A gig is roughly equivalent to 1000MB of data.

**CD-ROM:**
Compact Disk Read Only Memory. It can store up to 700MB of information compared to 1.4MB of memory on a high density floppy disk. "Read only" means you cannot record data.

**RAM:**
Random Access Memory. RAM is the space in the computer that stores the information you're working with at a particular moment.

is where your computer's operating system, programs, and other data files are stored. Hard drive space is measured in megabytes, often called "megs" and written as MB (as in 16MB, 64MB, and so forth). A megabyte is simply a standardized unit of measure. As programs become more powerful and complex, they require more hard drive space. A few years ago, 40MB of hard drive space was considered adequate. Today it's difficult to find a computer with less than 700MB; most come with between 2.1 and 9 **gigs** of hard drive. You can get on the Internet with as little as 40–80MB (assuming you have no other data files on your computer); however, if you plan to buy a new computer, I would recommend starting with around 2 gigs or more of hard drive space.

        **Memory.** There are actually two types of memory in your computer. The first is disk storage, such as the hard drive, **CD-ROM**, or floppy disk. The second is **RAM**. To explain the difference between the two, let's use an analogy from the human brain: Do you remember your first car? That's probably not something you thought about today, but with a little thinking you may be able to retrieve the information from your memory. All the information stored in your brain (like the memory of your first car) is like the information stored on a computer's hard drive. The computer isn't using this information all the time; but when it needs it, the computer can retrieve it. The RAM is the place *to which* the information is retrieved. (We say the memory of your first car "came to mind.") Data on your computer must be retrieved from the hard drive (or the CD-ROM, floppy drive, or the Internet) into the RAM for the microprocessor to be able to deal with it. The more RAM a computer has, the more information the processor has access to at one time. A large RAM capacity greatly increases the processing speed. All software lists a minimum amount of RAM required for a program to operate. Most Internet access software

**14**

packages require a minimum of 8MB of RAM. However, 16–32MB are much better.

**Modem.** The modem is the hardware that allows your computer to transfer information, including information from the Internet, over a copper telephone line. Like everything else on the computer, modems operate at a variety of speeds. Common modem speeds are 9,600 **baud**, 14,400 baud, 28,800 baud, 33,600 baud, and 56,000 baud. Modems can be internal or an external "stand-alone" unit; most new computers have internal modems. There are other ways to access the Internet besides using a modem, such as **ISDN**, Direct Satellite, and broadband cable. At the time of writing, cable access is being tested, and ISDN isn't available in all markets. These alternative ways to get on the Internet are too expensive for the average user; this is likely to change in the near future.

**All the Rest.** There are a few other items that can make your Internet experience more enjoyable. Although you don't need them, you may ultimately want speakers and a sound card. Many web pages include music or other sound files.

In terms of a monitor, a 14-inch VGA (Video Graphics Array) is probably the minimum you need. If you're buying new equipment, you certainly will want SVGA (Super Video Graphics Array). If it's in your budget, a 17-inch monitor is an excellent upgrade. There are also a variety of goodies that can accelerate the downloading of various files. You don't need any of these items to get online; however, if money is no object, they can enhance your experience of surfing the Internet.

### HOW DO I GET CONNECTED?

Once you have a computer that's capable of accessing the Internet, you need an avenue for that access. At this time, standard telephone lines

**BAUD:**
The term used for measuring the speed at which a modem operates. The higher the baud of your modem, the faster you will be able to access the Internet.

**ISDN:**
Integrated Services Digital Network. A way of accessing the Internet similar to a modem. ISDN uses existing phone lines and computer networks to deliver faster video, voice, and data transfer—up to 128 kilobits per second. It requires expensive hardware, and the fee for ISDN service is higher than for a modem.

**GRAPHICAL INTERFACE:**
Software using graphics and icons (pictures) instead of strings of complex computer coding.

**WEB BROWSER:**
Software that allows a user to view a web page and navigate among web pages and web sites on the World Wide Web.

**E-MAIL:**
Term used to describe messages that are sent and received electronically.

provide the access. The physical connection is simple. The modem has a jack just like the one on a telephone. Simply plug one end of the phone line into the jack on the modem, and plug the other end into the nearest telephone wall jack. All you need now is a service provider to help you access the Internet.

For the most part you have two choices. One option is to use a commercial online service, such as *America Online, CompuServe,* or *Prodigy.* The other option is to gain access through a true ISP. A little later we will discuss what these services offer; for now, the basic difference between a commercial online service and an ISP has to do with services provided, quality of access, and availability of local access. A commercial online service will have a user-friendly **graphical interface** that's simple to use. Typically, commercial online services include chat rooms for members, online news services, games, a built-in **web browser**, and a variety of other amenities. By contrast, an ISP usually provides a telephone number and a corresponding account that allows access to the Internet. You choose your own **e-mail** software and web browser. The major browsers at this time are *Netscape Navigator* and *Microsoft Internet Explorer.*

In deciding whether to go with a commercial online service or an ISP, there are a few things to consider. While a service like *America Online* is probably easier for a novice and offers more bells and whistles, the larger ISPs tend to offer faster, more reliable access.

The other important issue is local access. The commercial online services and the ISPs will offer a variety of phone numbers to access their service. Before signing on with any provider, check to be sure that it offers a number within your local calling area. Never sign on for Internet access through a long-distance number. The service charge paid to the provider covers only the cost of accessing the Internet, not long-distance (toll) time and charges. So you may spend only $20 a month for the online service, but you easily could spend $500 a month in toll charges reaching the service. The commercial online services tend to have local access numbers in every major market. However, if you're in an outlying community, you may have no choice but to go with an ISP to get a local access number.

Unless you install a separate phone line for a modem, your telephone will ring busy while you're online. If you're setting up Internet access at the church office, consider adding a separate phone line. "Call answering" is a less-expensive option if the church doesn't already have voice mail service. In "call answering," the telephone company provides an automated answering service for a nominal monthly fee (usually $3–$5). This service has a distinct advantage over an answering machine, since messages can be left even when the phone line is busy. So if you're online when people call, they can at least leave a message.

### HOW MUCH DOES IT COST TO BE ONLINE?

At this time, the standard monthly fee is $19.95 for unlimited Internet access. This means that, for a flat rate of about $20 a month, you can be online as much as you want. Some companies still offer metered plans (for example, $5 per month for the first 10 hours; then 50 cents for each additional hour).

I strongly recommend using an unlimited plan. Online time flies by quicker than you can imagine. Some ISPs provide slightly better rates for their metered plans. However, better rates often require a prepaid one- to three-year contract. It's probably a good idea to try a service for a month or two before entering into a long-term contract. Many online service providers offer a free trial period. If you're willing to go through the sign-up procedure several times, try as many online services as you can.

The only problem is that your e-mail address will change with each service. If you know you're only shopping around, don't share your e-mail address with too many people. They may become frustrated when they try to send e-mail, only to find that your e-mail address has changed.

If you live in a major Internet market area (such as a big city), you probably will have a number of service providers from which to choose. If you're fortunate enough to have several options, there are a few other things to consider:

• How many users are allowed on a single account? In other words, can each family member have his or her own e-mail address, or does everyone share a single address?

• Does the service provide space for you to post your own web site? We will talk about how to do this later.

• If the service does provide web space, how much is available? Two megabytes is minimum; 5MB is better; 10MB is very good for most applications.

• How often do users encounter busy signals? This is particularly important during peak hours when thousands of users are online. Some commercial online services have had significant problems in this area.

• What access speed to the Internet is available? Don't settle for less than 28,800 baud. The fastest modem on the market is worthless if your service provider is only offering access at 14,400 baud.

I hope this opening chapter has given you some understanding of what the Internet is and how it works. But there's much more to discover. In the next few chapters you will learn how the Internet can benefit the ministry of the church and the ministry of the individual Christian.

# *Getting Online:*

# What's in It for the Church?

In Chapter One we learned some of the history of the Internet; we gained some understanding of how it works; and we even began to learn the lingo and buzzwords of the Internet.

The question to consider in this chapter is, What's in it for the church? Is there any place for the Internet in the work of Christ's church? The answer is an unequivocal yes. In fact, within a few years, congregations that have failed to establish some kind of presence on the Internet will be at a distinct disadvantage. Twenty years ago many churches had no nursery. Of those that had a nursery, many were poorly maintained and less than inviting. Today a church that offers a clean, attractive, properly staffed nursery is at a distinct advantage. A church without a nursery still can be vital and growing, but a church that offers quality nursery care sends a clear message that it cares about young children and their parents.

**URL:**

Uniform Resource Locator. This is the address system used on the WWW. A URL is the string of letters, symbols, and punctuation a user must specify to reach a web page.

Likewise, churches with a presence on the Internet send a clear message. Today's children and youth are growing up with the Internet. Moreover, its use spans generational lines: Not only children, but also retirees and every age group in between, are becoming Internet users by the thousands. (Conservative estimates are that at least sixty million people worldwide are online.) People are using the Internet for everything from communication to commerce. Churches that are online and use e-mail send a message of relevance.

### WE ARE WITH YOU WHERE YOU ARE

IMHO, as we plunge headlong into the new millennium, one significant issue the church will struggle with is relevance. Much of our secular society sees the church as antiquated and irrelevant. And why wouldn't it? Many of us worship in buildings that are more than one hundred years old. Many churches have built their ministries on models from the 1950's. We sing hymns written hundreds of years ago, accompanied by a culturally outdated instrument, the organ. (When was the last time you heard an organ played on the radio?) It's not surprising that many people born after 1960 struggle to find relevance in the mainline church. And truthfully, many people of the baby-boom generation (born from 1946 to 1961) perceive the church in the same way.

Having a presence in cyberspace helps update the church's image. Before anyone ever sees a church's web page, the fact that it *has* one sends a message: It says to the unchurched, many of whom are online, that the church is active in contemporary society. Many people who aren't online (but will be someday) will notice that you're on the Internet. For this reason, once your congregation has established a web site and an e-mail address, it's important that you let people know. Your **URL** and e-mail address should be on your business cards, your church's letterhead, posters, press releases, and anywhere else you can make it visible to the public.

### GETTING TO KNOW US CAN BE FUN

Presenting an image of cultural relevance is just the beginning of the value of the Internet to the church. The Internet is quickly emerging as the most powerful marketing tool since television. However, before diving into how we use the Internet as a tool of marketing, we should say something about the issue of marketing and the church.

Some people think the church shouldn't be in the marketing business. I think this is because we often equate marketing with selling. Marketing is a tool of commercial sales, but its meaning and value go well beyond this. The key is to think about marketing as a tool. Tools can be used for good or for ill. The hammer that's used to build a home can be used to tear it down. The tools used to sell name-brand athletic shoes or to promote a political candidate can be used to share the gospel.

The fact is, most churches are involved in marketing efforts already. If you have a church sign, you are involved in marketing. If your worship service is announced in the newspaper, you're involved in marketing. If you have ever personally invited a friend or a neighbor to church, you're involved in marketing. Marketing is simply a way to help the church become known in the community. In his letter to the Romans, Paul asks: "But how are they to call on one in whom they have not believed? And how are they to believe in one of whom they have never heard?" (Romans 10:14).

The Internet is one tool through which the world may hear about the church and about the gift —the gospel of Jesus Christ—the church has to share. It's a tool, in the same way that the news-

**SERVER:**
Any computer that stores information and makes it available to outside users on a network.

**VIRTUAL:**
An environment created within a computer that to some degree imitates reality.

**HYPERLINK:**
Also called hypertext link; a spot on a web page that links the page to another web page, web site, or another place on the same page.

**BOOKMARK:**
A way of storing the location (URL) of a particular web page so that it can be easily retrieved later.

paper, television, radio, and direct mail are tools. It conveys information about your church and its ministries, and it can be an avenue to invite people to participate in those ministries.

Several things, however, set the Internet apart from other media in terms of its power as a marketing tool. The Internet offers marketing advantages that other media can't match. Consider the following:

**Information Galore**. The amount of information that can be posted on a web site is virtually unlimited. For the purpose of speedy downloading, there's a limit to the size a single web page ought to be. However, your web site can contain as many web pages as you wish. Commercial online services, such as *America Online,* will limit how many megabytes of web space you may post on their **server**. However, there are commercial web hosting companies that can provide as much space as you could possibly want. This means that you can describe every ministry your church offers in as much detail as you wish. Many church web sites post the pastor's sermon every week, providing an ongoing **virtual** library of sermons available to anyone. At the same time, a well-designed web site lets guests view only the information in which they are interested. With the appropriate use of **hyperlinks**, a user doesn't have to wade through a year's worth of sermons to discover the time of the Sunday morning worship service.

**Instant Availability**. A web site is available upon demand. Have you ever had the experience of hearing a radio commercial or seeing something on television that you wanted more information about? By the time you find a pencil and a piece of paper, the information is gone. Once a person has found your church's web site, he or she can **bookmark** it and return to it at any time. The person can read the information at his or her leisure, any time day or night. If something captures the person's interest,

he or she can print the information with a keystroke. With a minimum of effort, a user can provide all the information your church's web site has to offer by simply e-mailing the URL to a friend.

**Interactive Power**. One of the most exciting things about a web site is that it can be interactive. At the very least, most sites will include a link to e-mail the **webmaster** and the pastor. In that way, a guest reading through the church's web page can immediately e-mail someone at the church to request more information.

Another interactive feature found on many web sites is the guestbook. A guestbook allows the visitor to return information to the church within specifically defined parameters. Guestbooks have commonly been used to invite the visitors to respond to questions such as the following: "From what location are you contacting our web site?" "How did you like our web site?" Responses to such questions help the web site designer improve the web site.

The guestbook also can be used to share prayer requests or to accept registrations for vacation Bible school. The possibilities are limited only by the designer's imagination. Some of the more sophisticated, professionally designed commercial web sites make it possible not only for the guest and the web site sponsor to interact but also for the guest to interact with other guests. Much of this has become possible through the introduction of **Java**.

**Multimedia Possibilities**. Your web site can be not only interactive but can also have multimedia capabilities. Ever since the introduction of the WWW, it has been possible to view images. But now, through the use of **plug-ins**, most web browsers support both audio and video files. This means that hyperlinks can connect the viewer not only to other web pages but also to a variety of sound and full-motion video experiences. Your church's web

**WEBMASTER:**
The person responsible for maintaining a web site.

**JAVA:**
A programming language developed by Sun Microsystems and designed specifically for delivering applications on the Internet.

**PLUG-IN:**
Software that can be added to your browser to allow it to perform a specific function.

page can include a sound clip of the choir or an audio greeting from your pastor. It even could include a video clip from a sermon or church school activity. Unfortunately, because conveying motion and sound require huge files, multimedia on the Internet is somewhat limited at this time. However, as high-speed access becomes more widely available through cable or other technologies, the use of sound and video will become more prevalent.

**Low Cost**. As if all these advantages were not enough, consider the cost of marketing through the Internet. It's possible for a church to have a web site on the Internet at no cost. The General Board of Global Ministries is providing free web space for United Methodist congregations. There are a wide variety of other servers that provide free web space for churches. (See Chapter Six.)

Most of the servers providing free web space offer around 5MB. If this is not sufficient (as video and audio become more available, it probably will not be), there are commercial web site hosts offering space for a monthly fee. A typical deal might be $20 per month for 20–30MB of space, with additional space available as needed. Aside from unlimited space, the other advantage of renting space from a commercial host is that your church can have its own domain name. Twenty dollars a month is cheaper than a single newspaper advertisement. If your church is small and money is tight, you can still go with the free web space. Even 5MB is a lot of space if a web site consists primarily of text and a few pictures.

One final thought about marketing: A good marketing plan ought to include a variety of tools. The Internet is *one* tool; it is not intended to take the place of the congregation's other marketing efforts. Marketing tools such as press releases and newspaper advertisements, cable announcements, television and radio spots, public service announcements, signs, direct mail, and the Internet are most effective when they support one another. I encourage you to make sure your church has a unified approach to marketing that uses as many of these tools as possible.

One of the disadvantages of the Internet is that a web site sometimes can be difficult to find if a person does not know where to look. Most people will find your church's web site in one of two ways: through using a **search engine**, or by knowing the URL. People will know the URL because someone recommended it to them, or because they saw it somewhere (in the newspaper, on a sign, or on a piece of direct mail, for example). This is why a multifaceted marketing approach is so effective: Different tools (newspaper, direct mail, Internet) not only reach different people but the tools also reinforce one another.

### TALK IS EASY . . . AND CHEAP

Marketing is certainly an effective way for the church to use the Internet. Another important use is as a tool of communication. Actually, marketing itself is a form of communication. It is a way that businesses communicate with the outside world. But the Internet also can be used effectively for communication *within* the church. Used in this way, the Internet is not a tool for evangelism or outreach; it is a tool for aiding the flow of information within the congregation. If you've been involved in the church any time at all, you know how important internal communication can be.

Two forms of internal communication that the church can use exist on the Internet: the web site and e-mail. You can post information intended for the whole congregation on the church's web site, or you can use e-mail to communicate with specific individuals in the church. Posting information on the web site is similar to publishing the church's

**SEARCH ENGINE:**
A program that searches a collection of web pages for a specific key word (or words) a user has provided. Popular search engines include *Yahoo!, AltaVista, WebCrawler, HotBot, Lycos,* and *Excite.*

newsletter. The only difference is that you transfer the information electronically instead of through print.

Using the web site to distribute information has several advantages. For example, it

• eliminates postage costs;
• conserves natural resources by eliminating the use of paper;
• saves on the cost of labor (printing, collating, folding, and addressing the newsletter);
• sends the information instantly;
• allows you to communicate with as many people as you wish, including the general public, without increased cost;
• can be updated constantly.

Along with the types of information normally included in a newsletter, you may consider posting information such as the following:

• minutes of church meetings
• weekly prayer concerns mentioned during Sunday worship
• Scripture used in the sermon (for those who missed worship)
• a church calendar that can be updated as changes are made
• announcements of cancellations because of inclement weather (This information can be posted instantly, allowing people to check the web page before driving to a meeting or choir rehearsal unnecessarily.)
• announcements about a death in the community and about funeral arrangements

The obvious limitation to this form of communication is that it is available only to those members who have access to the Internet. At this point, that may be a small percentage of your congregation (although you might be surprised to find out how many members surf the Internet). Keep in mind, though, that people have access to the Internet not only at home but also at work, school, or even the local public library. You may find that the number of people in the church who have access to the Internet is higher than you thought. And you will almost certainly find that the number is increasing. However, there is still a need for printed communication. For the time being, sharing information through the church's web page is likely to be a supplement to, not a replacement of, the printed word.

The other form of internal communication is e-mail. Communicating through e-mail is similar to writing a letter or making a phone call. In many ways, e-mail has revived the art of letter writing. However, e-mail has a few advantages over the traditional letter. The first is that e-mail means instant communication. We don't always need instant communication, but sometimes it is helpful. I had an interesting Internet experience a few months ago. A Norwegian Methodist e-mailed me asking for my assistance. This person had a friend who lived in New Hampshire whom my Norwegian friend had not seen in some time. An opportunity arose for him to come to the United States from Norway on very short notice. He couldn't afford to visit the United States unless he could stay with his friend. Unfortunately, the man in Norway did not have his friend's unpublished phone number, only a mailing address. He knew that if he wrote the family, the letter would not get to the United States in time for him to book a flight. So he did a search on the Internet for United Methodist churches in New Hampshire and found my church's web site. He e-mailed me with the family's name and address, asking if I could deliver a message to the family. I didn't have time to drive out to the coast to deliver the message, so I accessed our annual conference's web page and pulled out the e-mail addresses of a few people who lived near the family the man was hoping to reach. I **forwarded** the message from Norway to

**FORWARD:**
A function of e-mail software that allows a user to pass on an e-mail message to one or more people.

all of them, hoping that one of them might be able to help. Within a few hours I got word back from one of the people I had e-mailed: This person had a friend (who was also online) who knew the family we were trying to reach. By that evening all the arrangements had been made for the Methodist from Norway to visit his friend in New Hampshire. My part in this was that it took me fifteen minutes to read, reply to, and forward the message!

Besides instant communication, e-mail offers other advantages too. Consider these:

• E-mail is free. That is to say, there is no charge beyond the flat-rate access fee you pay to the ISP for Internet access.

• E-mail is convenient. There is no searching for paper, pen, envelope, stamps, and address.

Now, I am sure some of you are thinking, *But what about the telephone?* The telephone is free (at least for local calls), and the telephone is convenient. But e-mail has a few advantages even over the telephone.

First, e-mail is not intrusive. One of the things people don't like about the telephone is that it can be intrusive. When the phone rings, you have to stop what you're doing and answer the call. E-mail, on the other hand, can be read at a time that is convenient for the recipient.

Second, e-mail messages can be more detailed than a message on an answering machine. Because the telephone is intrusive, many people now use their answering machines to screen their calls. If your experience is similar to mine, these days you end up talking more to answering machines than to people. E-mail allows you to leave a detailed, thought-out message.

Third, think cost again. Yes, the telephone is free (once you pay for your monthly service), but only for local calls. With e-mail you can communicate around the world at no additional charge. This is a tremendous blessing for families spread across the country. What's more, college students can e-mail home for money without their parents incurring the additional cost of a collect call!

Fourth, e-mail can be sent at any time. As a rule, I don't call people before 9:00 A.M. or after 9:00 P.M., but I often e-mail people at midnight. I can get up early in the morning, read my e-mail, and make my replies before many people are even awake. I could never do that with a telephone.

Fifth, e-mail is easily shared. Forwarding allows the recipient of an e-mail message to pass the message along to one or one hundred people quite easily. Forwarding is especially popular with good jokes. If a good joke hits the Internet, you can be pretty sure that within a few days, half of the Internet community will have seen it.

The important question here is, How should the church use e-mail? It should use e-mail in essentially the same ways that it would use letters or the telephone. Many of the same kinds of items that you would post on a church's web page also can be e-mailed to people affected by a particular item. For example, you might post an upcoming committee meeting on the web page. Following the meeting you might e-mail the minutes to committee members. Through the use of **attachments**, e-mail becomes an especially powerful tool. Attachments can transfer a document as fast as a fax; but unlike a fax, you can import a file attached to an e-mail message directly into a word processor, spreadsheet, or other software for immediate use and revision. My church does not have a paid secretary. We don't even have the space for a secretary to work. (We've converted all available space into educational space.) However, we do have two wonderful volunteers who work out of their homes. Each of them is online. Through the use of e-

**ATTACHMENT:**
A graphic, video, sound, or text file attached to an e-mail correspondence.

mail and attachments, we are able to work together as if we were all in the same building.

## NO EXCUSE NOT TO GROW

Another valuable function of the Internet for the church is in providing resources for church members (and others) for spiritual growth and discipleship. For example, many churches and Christian ministries now offer online Bible studies. A well-designed web site will have links to a variety of resources for Christian theology, Bible study tools, helps for sermon preparation, daily devotionals, and so forth. Through the use of these resources, congregations can help their members grow in Christian discipleship.

In the next chapter we will focus on the individual Christian and how the Internet can help him or her grow in faith.

# *Getting Online:*

# What's in It for the Individual Christian?

In the previous chapter we considered ways that the Internet can help ministry in the local church. In this chapter we look at how the individual Christian can benefit from the resources of the Internet.

Broadly speaking, the individual believer can use the Internet for two purposes: to communicate and to find and use resources.

## REACHING OUT AND TOUCHING ... EVERYONE
### *Newsgroups*

Individuals can communicate on the Internet in a variety of ways. One way is through **newsgroups**. Newsgroups are online discussion groups that allow the expression of a broad range of ideas and opinions. Newsgroups dedicated to the exchange of Christian ideas are probably not as pop-

**NEWSGROUP:**
A discussion group on the Internet allowing open exchange of ideas around a specific subject or subjects.

31

**POSTING:**
Leaving a message on a newsgroup.

**CHAT ROOM:**
A forum for real-time (live) discussion with other Internet users.

ular as some other newsgroups, such as *Star Trek* or *The X-Files*. Still, Christian newsgroups do receive their share of **postings**.

One drawback to this form of communication is that, like the Internet itself, it is wide open. Most newsgroups are unmoderated, allowing anyone to say anything he or she wishes. In this free exchange, one often finds obscenity, and even hostility toward Christianity. In this regard, newsgroups are similar to some call-in radio programs, except that newsgroups have no censor button. However, for those who like the challenge, it is a great place to share one's Christian witness.

### Chat Rooms

Another way to communicate on the Internet is the **chat room**. Chat rooms can be interesting because you have the opportunity to meet people from across the country and around the world. Unlike newsgroups, the conversations in a chat room happen in real time—they are live. Fortunately, it seems as though chat rooms are more likely to be monitored, especially chat rooms specifically for children. Unfortunately, chat rooms have been greatly abused. When you are communicating with others in a chat room—even a chat room sponsored by a Christian individual or group—use common sense. Don't give out personal information such as your full name or address. Remember that the Internet affords everyone total anonymity. The 45-year-old homemaker you are chatting with may really be a 15-year-old boy!

### E-mail

Certainly the most popular form of communication on the Internet is e-mail. Unlike newsgroups or chat rooms, e-mail involves direct communication with a specific individual. We talked about the benefits and value of e-mail in Chapter Two. But there are some specific ways that individuals can use e-mail. Think about these:

• Send e-mail to students from your church who are away at college. College students are not always the most disciplined about writing letters, but many of them read and write e-mail daily.

• Use e-mail to consult. United Methodists have a wide variety of resourceful people at jurisdictional and general agency levels. However, most of us, both pastors and laity, never communicate directly with any of them, often because we do not know their phone numbers or addresses. Or we don't want to bother these people because we consider our inquiry to be relatively minor. Many of these people have personal e-mail addresses. Since e-mail is less intrusive than a phone call, why not send your inquiry via e-mail? This way, the person has the time to prepare a thoughtful response at his or her leisure. In writing this book, I was able to communicate with a number of national-level consultants and denominational executives whom I probably never would have contacted over the telephone.

• Use e-mail to do committee work. If all, or most, of the members of a committee are online, much of the business of that committee can be handled via e-mail. Questions and responses can be sent to the chairperson; he or she can then forward the information instantly to all the other committee members. E-mail doesn't replace the need for committee meetings, but it does help keep information flowing smoothly between meetings. It also helps make committee meetings more productive, since members have the information they need in advance. Using e-mail in this way can be helpful in a local church setting; it is even more productive and cost-effective for committees and ministry teams at district or conference levels.

**HTTP:**

Hypertext Transfer Protocol. The protocol used to transfer HTML documents across the World Wide Web. The WWW can use other protocols as well, such as Gopher and FTP.

### Personal Web Pages

Another way to communicate on the Internet is to design and post a personalized web page. (See Chapter Four.) Just as a church web page shares information about the life and ministry of the congregation, so your personal web page can share valuable knowledge and information with others. As a pastor or layperson, you may have experience and knowledge about a particular area of ministry that could be of great benefit to others. Posting this information on your web page not only allows other believers to strengthen their ministries but also often leads to building important networks for sharing and receiving insights and ideas about a particular area of ministry. You may soon find yourself making contacts and even friendships throughout the country with people of similar interests and needs. For this networking to happen, include your e-mail address on your web page.

### Videoconferencing

Videoconferencing is another tool of communication that the Internet allows. With the right software and some fairly inexpensive accessories, you can do videoconferencing for free over the Internet. If you don't mind black and white images, you can be set up for under $100. The only drawback to this form of communication is that all the participants in the conference must have compatible software. As yet there is not a standard platform for videoconferencing. For the best results, all participants will want to have matching software. One particularly popular software is *CU-SeeMe*, which offers trial software. *Location:* **http://www.wpine.com/Products/CU-SeeMe**

### ALL THE HELP YOU WILL EVER NEED

The amount of information available on the Internet almost defies imagination. The following are some of the types of resources available that might be of interest to Christians.

### Personal Devotions

Hundreds of excellent web sites are available for personal devotional use. Many of these sites post a daily devotion; others post a weekly or monthly devotion. Some devotions are posted on a web page for you to look up; other sites will e-mail the devotion directly to you free of charge, if you sign up on the mailing list.

### Bible Study

The amount of information in this area is staggering, but the web sites generally fall into two categories. There are online Bible studies that allow you to study at home as part of a "cyber class." Other web sites contain resources to help you prepare to lead a Bible study. You will find everything from outlines to complete lesson plans that can be downloaded for free.

### Sermon Preparation

Like the Bible study web sites, a large number of sites exist to assist with sermon preparation. Many sites follow the Lectionary; others go by specific topics for sermons. Some of the sites offer a basic outline; others post the complete manuscript of a sermon. You also can find sites that allow you to exchange with other pastors ideas related to the upcoming Lectionary readings.

### Worship preparation

Some web sites go beyond helping you prepare sermons. These sites also offer ideas and suggestions about liturgy, music, drama, and all the other aspects needed to prepare a total worship experience.

**35**

**FREEWARE:**

Software that can be downloaded and used free of charge.

**SHAREWARE:**

Software that can be used free on a trial basis. After the trial period, if the user decides to keep the software, he or she pays a registration fee.

**ENCRYPTION:**

A way to secure data sent over the Internet to prevent unauthorized viewing. Encryption is most commonly used for online commerce, such as purchasing an item with a credit card.

### How-to Resources

A number of web pages are available that could best be described as "how-to" pages. These are often posted by individuals or churches who have successfully navigated a particular transition in ministry. Examples of such pages might be "How we started a second worship service" or "How we turned our youth ministry around." The pages often may not be as specific as the above examples; but if you find a church that has had real success in a particular area of ministry, a review of its web page and a follow-up e-mail inquiry can get you a lot of information.

### Free Software

Another wonderful resource you will find on the Internet is **freeware** or **shareware**. A few major web sites have large repositories of freeware or shareware. Most of these sites have a built-in search engine that allows you to search for the kind of software you want. Such a search generally will show a list of software options, each with a description and a rating of each option. Often the web site will state the number of times a particular software has been downloaded from the site. This is usually a good indication of the better software packages.

### Online Shopping

Another emerging resource on the Internet is online shopping. **Encryption** is now commonplace on the Internet, allowing for safe commerce in cyberspace. Online shopping is similar to buying items from a catalog or from a home shopping network. Christian resources are as plentiful in cyberstores as anything else.

### News

In conveying news, the Internet combines the benefits of the newspaper and of television. Like television, the Internet allows for instant

access to news, sports, weather, stocks, and much more. And like print media, the Internet allows users to go beyond the typical television sound bite to read in-depth reports. It also allows users to store, retrieve, and print information at will.

With more than 50,000,000 web pages worldwide, the trick is to find the information you want. Chapters Five and Six give you some places to start. From there you can follow the Web to other interesting and exciting sites. If you still don't find what you're looking for, you can always use a search engine.

### Why Pull If You Can Push?

Most resources on the Internet require you to seek out the information you need by scanning web pages or by using a search engine. The one important exception to that is **push** technology.

Push technology gained popularity in early 1996 with the release of *PointCast*. *PointCast* delivers news, sports, and weather information directly to the desktop of subscribers at chosen times each day. Since it was first introduced, a number of new push services have emerged with greater degrees of flexibility. What makes the newest versions of these push services so powerful is that they allow you, the end user, to determine what type of information you want sent to you. The service then searches the Internet constantly for information and news that meets your specifications.

These services vary greatly in terms of how specific you can make a search. Moreover, the information is delivered in a variety of ways. Some use a "ticker-type" display across the top or bottom of the computer screen; others have an icon that pops up when new information has been found. Still others allow you to retrieve the information at your leisure, much the way you would check your e-mail or a spe-

**PUSH:**
Push services allow information to be sent directly to your computer according to predetermined specifications.

cific web page. The best part is that these services are generally free. They are funded by advertising income from banner advertisements.

Quite a number of push services are available, but a handful seem to stand above the rest. They include

• **PointCast Network**
Location: *http://www.pointcast.com*
• **BackWeb**
Location: *http://www.backweb.com*
• **Castanet**
Location: *http://www.marimba.com*
• **Intermind Communicator**
Location: *http://www.intermind.com*
• **Headliner Professional**
Location: *http://www.lanacom.com*

Of the above, *Headliner Professional* seems to offer the most power and flexibility.

The Internet: What's in it for you? There is lots in it for you. The Internet is not only a great way to have fun but is also a powerful tool for strengthening your ministry and for growing in faith.

# *Finding a Place in Cyberspace:*

# How to Design Your Own Web Page

Once you have begun to explore the World Wide Web, you almost certainly will want a web site of your own. At last count a little more than one thousand United Methodist Church web sites were linked on the General Board of Global Ministries' list of local church home pages.

In this chapter we will explore how you and your church can develop a web site, post it on the Internet, and promote it. If you are truly new to the world of the Internet, this will sound like a daunting job. However, it is easier than you think. What's more, the only cost may be the time you choose to invest! It's possible to spend a lot of money designing, posting, and promoting a web site, but it's not necessary.

## GET READY, GET SET ...

A walk through any large secular bookstore will reveal an entire aisle of books related to

**HTML:**
Hypertext Markup Language. This is the code used for writing most web pages.

the Internet. Many of them are instructional manuals about designing a web site. This brief chapter is not intended to replace those resources; however, it will give you a basic understanding of how **HTML** works, as well as give you the information you need to construct a basic web page. If you want to get into the finer details of HTML programming, do further research—not in a bookstore but on the Internet.

There are thousands of web sites that explain everything from "image mapping" to "animated GIF construction" to "Java script." This chapter covers the basics in plain English for those of us who are "technologically challenged."

Dozens of excellent programs are on the market that can help you construct a web page. Some of the programs assist you in working directly in HTML. Essentially they save you some typing by putting HTML tags in place with the click of a mouse. Others, however, do everything for you; you don't need any knowledge of HTML at all. Although these programs are fast, powerful, and convenient, they are often expensive. Furthermore, you learn to rely on the program and never really learn to use HTML. This is a problem when it is time to update your web site (which ought to happen regularly), because it is generally easier to work directly with the source code. However, you cannot work with source code if you don't understand it. What's more, if you understand how HTML works, you are able to learn from others. If you discover something that you like on another web page, you can use it because you can read the source code and understand how it was done.

Whether you intend to use HTML software or not, I would encourage you to design your very first page from scratch without the help of a software package. Then you will have some understanding of how a web page works.

**GO!**

As you may recall, HTML stands for **Hypertext** Markup Language. Although it can be considered a programming language, HTML does not begin to approach the complexity of other computer programming languages now in use. It uses only the plain text, numbers, characters, and punctuation that you see on your keyboard. It is called a "markup" language because it uses special markup codes mixed in directly with the text to tell the browser how to display the text, where to place a graphic, or when to play a sound file. These <bracketed> markup codes are visible in your HTML document as you are creating it. When the page is viewed through a web browser, the markup codes are not displayed. The codes direct how the text, graphics, and hyperlinks should be displayed on the page. Below is an example of the source code for the most basic HTML document.

**HYPERTEXT:**
Hypertext is a word, or words, appearing in a color different from the rest of the text on a web page. Hypertext acts as a hyperlink.

```
<HTML>
<HEAD>
<TITLE>My First Web Page</TITLE>
</HEAD>
<BODY>
<H1><CENTER>Pastor Steve's Basic Web Page
</CENTER></H1>
<BR>
While simple, this displays the fundamental principles
upon which a web page is built.
</BODY>
</HTML>
```

The document would look like this when viewed through your web browser:

```
Pastor Steve's Basic Web Page
While simple, this displays the fundamental
principles upon which a web page is built.
```

**TAG:**

Tags are markup code words inside angle brackets. For example, <CENTER>, <H1>.

The title, "My First Web Page," appears in the title bar of the page, but does not display in the document itself.

Even from this simple source code, you can see some of the important basic principles of HTML. First, note that the items in the angle brackets (< >) are not displayed. Second, you probably saw that the **tags** all came in pairs. This is not always the case. Some markup codes do not require a closing tag, but the majority of them do. Closing tags have a forward slash mark ( / ) in front of the text within the brackets. It is best that a beginner use pairs. If a closing tag is required, but you forget to put it in, you will see an error when you view the document. On the other hand, the browser will ignore unnecessary closing tags. You may have noticed that the letters within the brackets are all capitals. Since tags are not case-sensitive, it is not necessary to use capital letters; however, using capital letters is generally considered to be good form. Using capital letters in your tags makes it easier to distinguish the content of the web page from the markup language.

As mentioned earlier, the closing tags all include a forward slash between the first angle bracket and the first letter. For example </HTML>, </CENTER>, and so forth are closing tags. Once your browser finds an opening tag, it will treat all the text that follows it according to the direction in the tag until it finds a closing tag. For example, if I had neglected the closing </CENTER> tag on the first line, it would have centered all the text that followed.

Another thing that you can do to make HTML easier to view and to work with is to add space where you like. You can have lots of space between paragraphs in the source document, but that same space will not be in the HTML document. As we will see later, you have to add tags for paragraphs and line breaks—otherwise, the text will all run together.

You may have noticed that the <HTML> tag opens the document, and the </HTML> tag closes the document. These tags are a required part of the source code. They declare that this is an HTML document and that it should be read as such.

Note that there are two parts to an HTML document: the heading and the body. The heading contains the title and sometimes other information related to the document. The information in the <HEAD> portion of the document is not displayed on the viewed page. This is why the information between the <TITLE> tags, "My First Web Page," is not displayed in our example. Therefore, every page begins with this basic shell from which you will work:

```
<HTML>
<HEAD>
<TITLE></TITLE>
</HEAD>
<BODY>
</BODY>
</HTML>
```

Now at this point you may be wondering: *If I'm not going to buy some expensive HTML software program, how do I record and store the information I create for my web page?* The answer is simple: Since HTML is plain text, or **ASCII** language, you can use any text editor you wish. If you are using Windows 95, the easiest thing to use is the notepad found under "Accessories." (The instructions in this book are for PCs; instructions for Macs may differ.) Simply open the notepad and begin typing. If you don't have a notepad, any text editor will work fine. You can even use your desktop publishing software if it includes an option that allows you to work in ASCII format rather than **WYSIWYG**. When you're ready to save the file, you can use any extension you want.

**ASCII:**
American Standard Code for Information Interchange—an ASCII file contains standard text characters as data. This standardized format allows text files to be shared across various software formats.

**WYSIWYG:**
What You See Is What You Get —WYSIWYG displays text on your computer screen just as it will appear on the printed page. For example, bolded text will look bold; centered text will be centered.

**HOME PAGE:**
The term has two meanings, depending on how it's used. Any person can have a "home page." Such a page usually contains personal information about the person and his or her work. "Home page" also refers to the first page of a multipage web site. This type of "home page" would act like a table of contents with multiple hyperlinks leading to more in-depth information.

However, it is good practice to use the extension ".htm" (or ".html," if you are able to have long extensions), so that you can identify it later as an HTML document. The earlier sample document might be saved as "stevedoc.htm."

Because HTML is a markup language, and not WYSIWYG, you will want to preview your document from time to time as you are working on it. To do this, follow these easy steps:

1. Open your browser (such as *Netscape Navigator* or *Microsoft Internet Explorer*). You don't have to be online to do this.

2. Under the "File" menu, click "Open File" (or the similar command in your browser).

3. Work your way through the directory until you find the saved file.

4. Click on "OK" to open the file. (If your hard drive looks anything like mine, it may be easier to locate the document if you saved it on a floppy disk.)

### THERE'S NO TIME LIKE THE PRESENT

Why don't you take a break right now and try your hand at designing your very own web page? If your plan is to create a web page for your church, you might as well start right now by practicing with a basic outline for that page. This will be a good opportunity to learn more about HTML. You can use the simple web page you will be creating in a few moments as the framework from which to support the expanded web page.

Follow these basic steps:

1. Open your text editor.

2. Create the basic framework for the web page, and insert the following text:

**\<HTML\>**
**\<HEAD\>**
**\<TITLE\>**My Church **Home Page\</TITLE\>**

```
</HEAD>
<BODY>
<H1><STRONG><CENTER>Welcome to Christ Is
Lord United Methodist Church Home Page
</CENTER></STRONG></H1>
<HR>
```

Insert some basic information here, such as the church's mission statement, times of worship, address, phone number, and so forth.

```
</BODY>
</HTML>
```

3.  Save the file to a floppy disk as "mychurch.htm" or any other appropriate file name.
4.  Open your web browser and follow the steps on page 44 for previewing the document.

How did it come out? Did you figure out that the <HR> tag represents a horizontal rule? The page probably looks okay, but not too exciting. So let's explore some ways to "jazz up" the page a little. As we look at some neat ways to improve the look of your web page, remember that HTML is continually being improved to make possible greater flexibility in formatting web pages. As HTML evolves, and as you do your own research beyond the basics described here, you will be able to do much more.

### HAVE FUN WITH FORMATS

Before getting into graphics, let's take a look at what can be done with the text of the web page itself. Tags allow you to format the text in a variety of ways. When you look at the document above, you will see several text-formatting tags.

**Headline Tags**. The size of the text can be adjusted by using headline tags, ranging from <H1> to <H6>. <H1> represents the largest type size available; <H6> is the smallest.

**Bold Tags.** Any text appearing between the <STRONG> </STRONG> tags will be in boldface.

**Italics Tags.** Any text appearing between the <EM> </EM> tags will be italicized.

**Centering Tags.** Any text appearing between the <CENTER> </CENTER> tags will be centered on the page.

You can also determine the layout of the page through the use of tags. You may recall that the browser ignores any white space in the source document. This does not mean that it is not possible to have white space between lines of text; it simply means that you must tell the browser when to insert the spacing. You do this with a <P> (paragraph) tag. The <P> tag will put a blank line between the text before and after it. You can use multiple <P> tags to create a wider space.

Your browser also ignores any "carriage returns" (new paragraph symbols) that show on your source document. In other words, even if you hit the Return key between two lines of text while typing the source document, your browser will still put the text on the same line—unless you specifically instruct the browser to place the text on the next line. This is done with a <BR> (line break) tag. The difference between a line break and a paragraph tag is that the line break will simply space down; it will not leave a blank space. Neither the <P> nor the <BR> requires closing tags. When I created the simple document on page 45, the heading broke between "Methodist" and "Church," simply because that is the point at which it ran out of space. It would have been more attractive had I done the following:

**<H1><STRONG><CENTER>**Welcome to Christ Is Lord**<BR>**United Methodist Church Home Page**</CENTER></STRONG></H1>**

Now it would display like this:

**Welcome to Christ Is Lord
United Methodist Church Home Page**

Or I could have done this:

**<H1><STRONG><CENTER>**Welcome to**<P>**Christ
Is Lord**<BR>**United Methodist Church Home Page
**</CENTER></STRONG></H1>**

The result would be:

**Welcome to**

**Christ Is Lord
United Methodist Church Home Page**

### DON'T FORGET TO MAKE A LIST

The other formatting tool you may want to use on your web page is the list. There are several types of lists, and you can mix them in a variety of ways. However, for the sake of simplicity, we will look at the three basic types of lists:

• unordered (bulleted)
• ordered (numbered)
• menu (stacked)

To create a list in HTML, you will combine two different tags. The first set of tags, which are placed at the beginning and end of the list, specifies what type of list it is: <UL> </UL> is an unordered list; <OL> </OL> is an ordered list; and <MENU> </MENU> is a stacked list (indented and without numbers or bullets). Each item in any of these lists must then have the <LI> (list item) tag before it. Here is an example of an unordered list:

At our church, we offer the following ministries:
**<BR>**
**<UL>**

```
<LI>Sunday School
<LI>Choir
<LI>Youth Group
<LI>Adult Bible Study
</UL>
```

When displayed, it looks like this:

```
At our church, we offer the following
ministries:
    • Sunday School
    • Choir
    • Youth Group
    • Adult Bible Study
```

Notice that the closing tag is necessary only at the end of the whole list, not after individual items. This is because the next open <LI> tag indicates the start of a new item; therefore, it obviously also indicates the end of the previous item.

### PICTURE THIS!

Experimenting with text size and layout will add a little life to your web page. However, it has been the introduction of images to web pages that has made the WWW so popular. One important word of caution: Be judicious about introducing images to your web page; they can take quite a while to download. The day is coming when download speeds will be so fast that even full-motion video will not be a problem. Unfortunately, we're not there yet. It will be some time before high-speed access is available to most Internet users. For that reason be conservative with the number and size of the images you introduce to your web page. Always keep in mind that the larger (the more KBs) the page, the longer it will take to download. If your page takes very long to download, most Internet surfers will leave without ever seeing it (or will get annoyed at how long you made them wait).

Most web site designers will have a very "lean" front page. This allows the viewer rapid access to the web site. Once in, the viewer can be linked to many pages. A good rule of thumb is to design a front page with very few images; the page should download in less than thirty seconds. For the rest of your web site, try to strike an appropriate balance between visually attractive pages and reasonable download times. Often this will mean spreading images over several linked pages, even if the images are all related to the same ministry, event, or subject. Most graphics (clip art) are designed to use as little computer memory as possible. It is often **digitized photographs** that consume large amounts of memory and download time. Most images on the Internet come in one of two formats: **GIF** or **JPEG**.

Images on the Internet can be used in a variety of ways. Here are some:

**Background.** As you surf the Internet, you will notice that some people's web pages have a solid white or colored background; other pages have some kind of background design or pattern. This is done by adding the following <BODY> tag within the command line: BACKGROUND=YOUPICK.GIF. Therefore, it would look like this: <BODY BACKGROUND=YOUPICK.GIF>. Of course, the name of the GIF file you choose will replace the letters "YOUPICK.GIF."

**Graphics.** You probably will want to add digitized photographs, clip art, colored bars, shapes, and buttons to your web page. To place these images in the page, you use the <IMG> tag with the appropriate **attributes**. At a bare minimum, the <IMG> tag must include the SRC attribute (specifies the source of the image; that is, the file in which the image is found). It is also good form to include the ALT attribute (provides a description of the image while the image is downloading). Thus, a basic image com-

**DIGITIZED PHOTOGRAPH:**
Digitizing is the process of converting a visual image into bits of computer data, allowing an image to be stored or manipulated digitally.

**GIF:**
Graphics Interchange Format. A ".gif" extension (for example, "cross.gif") indicates that the file contains some kind of graphic— a picture, photo, clip art, or other image.

**JPEG:**
Joint Photographic Experts Group. JPEG files have the extension ".jpg" or ".jpeg" (for example, "church.jpg"). MPEG is the movie counterpart to JPEG.

**ATTRIBUTES:**
Commands that affect the appearance of the image to which they are attached.

mand would look something like this: <IMG ALT="[Church Picture]" SRC="MYCHURCH.GIF">. Attributes also can be used to adjust the size and alignment of the images. If you do not specify an alignment of the image, the browser will align the bottom of the image with the bottom of the text where the <IMG> tag appears in the source code.

**Animated GIFs**. Animated GIFs are files that incorporate a series of pictures that, when displayed in succession, create the illusion of movement. You can insert animated GIFs in your web page by using the same command line as a regular GIF or JPEG image.

The question now becomes: Where do you get all these images? Images for your web page can be secured in a number of ways. First, you can purchase a disk of web graphics. Such a disk generally includes a variety of backgrounds, lines, bars, and clip art images. Second, by searching around, you are likely to find web sites that allow you to download image files for free. For example, the General Board of Global Ministries of The United Methodist Church has a collection of images that can be downloaded for free at *http://gbgm-umc.org/docs/graphics.html/*. Third, with permission, you often can copy backgrounds, or any other image, directly from any web page. This is amazingly easy to do. And because it is so easy, it has become commonplace on the Internet. However, before explaining how it is done, we must address the issue of copyright.

## LIVE UNDER THE LAW

Everything on the Internet was created by someone. As such, it is the property of the individual or company that created it. In earlier days of software development, people caught on pretty quickly that it was possible for one person to purchase a piece of software and then to make copies of it for his or her friends. While it was easy, it was neither legal nor moral. When photocopiers became a common piece of equipment for most church offices, music directors were able to purchase a single piece of music and copy it for every member of the choir. Again, this practice was both illegal and immoral.

With a click of a mouse button, images, source codes, scripts, backgrounds, sound files, video, and more can be immediately transferred from the page you are viewing to your hard drive to be used as you wish. However, like a piece of music or a software program, those items belong to someone else. This does not mean that we can never "borrow" from someone else's page. What it means is that *before* we do, we need to secure permission. Quite often, the e-mail address of the webmaster is posted at the bottom of the page. Unless the page specifically states that the images (code, script, and so forth) are free for the taking, you must contact the webmaster for permission to copy anything. The granting of such permission is common in the Internet community. If you are borrowing extensively from a particular site, you should acknowledge that. The acknowledgment can be listed in the source code, or it may be done by providing a **link** to that person's page.

As Christians we ought to be setting the standard with regard to copyright. What kind of a witness is it to the Internet community for a church to build its web page out of stolen building blocks? The question is not whether or not we will get caught; the question is whether or not it is right. Many people will be honored to share their work with you. But ask first.

### NOW, BACK TO THE DRAWING BOARD

After you have secured permission to borrow a background or other image, here is how you copy an image. (The process varies somewhat among browsers, but not much.)

**LINK:**
A connection that takes the viewer from one web page to another. This is generally done with a hyperlink.

Begin by clicking with the right mouse button on the image you want to copy. A box will pop up with several options. Choose "Save As." A second box will appear with a suggested destination for the file and a suggested name. You can change the destination if you want it stored in a different place, and you can rename the file if you wish (although the GIF or JPG extension must remain the same). Click on "OK," and the image is yours.

If you have secured permission to use someone's source code, you would follow a similar procedure. First, you must view the source code. Go to the "View" menu and select "Source Code." It is easiest to highlight the portion of the source code you want to save, then cut it to the clipboard. Later, paste the borrowed source code from the clipboard into your HTML document for the appropriate modifications. If your browser won't allow you to do this, you can generally go to the "File" menu and use the "Save As" function to save the entire document. You can then open the file with your text editor and lift out the portions of the source code that you need.

So let's try adding an image or two to our document. Go to the General Board of Global Ministries' web site at *http://gbgm-umc.org/GIFS/* and copy several of the GIF files for use during this exercise. Now, go back to your basic HTML document and make the following changes to turn the text into boldface:

**<HTML>**
**<HEAD>**
**<TITLE>**My Church Home Page**</TITLE>**
**</HEAD>**
**<BODY BACKGROUND=**"[*Insert a GIF file here*]">
**<H1><STRONG><CENTER><IMG SRC=**"[*Insert a GIF file here*]"
**ALIGN=**"**left**">Welcome**<P><H4>**to**</H4>**Christ Is

Lord**\<BR\>**United Methodist Church Home Page
**\</CENTER\>\</STRONG\>\</H1\>**
**\<HR\>**
Insert some basic information here, such as your mission statement, times of worship, address, phone number, and so forth.
**\<P\>**At our church we offer the following ministries:
**\<OL\>**
**\<LI\>**Sunday School
**\<LI\>**Choir
**\<UL\>\<LI\>**Cherubs**\<LI\>**Youth**\<LI\>**Adults**\</UL\>**
**\<LI\>**Youth Group
**\<LI\>**Adult Bible Study
**\</OL\>**
**\</BODY\>**
**\</HTML\>**

### GET HYPER ABOUT LINKS

Even in the most basic web page design, there is still one more item that we need to discuss: hyperlinks. Even the most elementary web page is likely to include one or two links. Links are created through the use of an \<A\> (anchor) tag. Anchor tags take a viewer to another spot on the same web page or to another web page. For the sake of simplicity, we will concern ourselves with linking two web pages.

The basic anchor tag would look something like this: \<A HREF="destination"\>"clickable text"\</A\>. The portion marked "destination" designates the name of the HTML file to which you are linking. If it is a file within your own web site, it need only include the file name; if it is a link to someone else's web site, it would include the entire URL. The second portion of the anchor tag (labeled "clickable text") indicates a space to insert any words you wish. Text inserted here will appear on the viewed web page as highlighted text. The viewer clicks on this highlighted

**THUMBNAIL:**
A low-resolution, down-sized version of a digital image. Many sites allow a viewer to see the full-size image by clicking on the thumbnail image.

text with the mouse pointer to be taken to the linked page.

Here are a couple of examples:

*Example 1:*
**<A HREF="page2.htm">**Click here to see page two**</A>**

*Example 2:*
**<A HREF="http://www.stmattumc.org">**Click here to go to St. Matthews Web Page**</A>**

The link in the first example would take the viewer to the second page in your own web site (named "page2.htm"). The link in the second example would take the viewer to the web page for St. Matthews United Methodist Church in Sandown, New Hampshire. By the way, the phrase "Click here to go to" is generally not necessary; most Web surfers would know that "St. Matthews UMC" in highlighted text represents a link to that web page.

It is possible to use an image as a hyperlink. When the viewer clicks on the image, he or she is taken to the linked web page or web site. Graphics are often used to give the viewer a clue about the kind of web site or page he or she is about to link to. For example, a picture of a mailbox may represent e-mail, or a **thumbnail** may represent a photograph.

To use an image as a hyperlink, simply place the <IMG> tag in place of, or along with, the clickable text. Here is an example:

**<A HREF="sanctry.htm"><IMG SRC="thumb-nal. gif">**>View our Sanctuary**</A>**

This command takes the viewer to a page that includes a picture ("sanctry.gif") of your sanctuary (and any text you care to add around it). You also could take the viewer directly to the image with no page built around it by changing the HREF like this:

**\<A HREF="sanctry.gif">\<IMG SRC="thumb-nal. gif">**View our Sanctuary**\</A>**

One other anchor you will want to know about is the "mail to" command. This anchor allows you to have a hyperlink on your page that takes viewers directly to an e-mail screen with your church's e-mail address in the "mail to" box. At the very least, you will want to have an e-mail link to the person maintaining your web page. This allows viewers to ask questions or to report problems with the page. The anchor for an e-mail link would look like this:

**\<A HREF="MAILTO:stmattumc@aol.com">**E-mail Pastor Steve**\</A>**

### BUT WAIT, THERE'S MORE
There are many other things that you can do to make a web page exciting, interesting, and helpful. After you have mastered the basics covered in this chapter, do some more research on your own. As I mentioned earlier, the easiest way to do this kind of research is to use the Internet itself.

Here are a few key words that you might want to look up on your favorite search engine:
- HTML Tables
- HTML Frames
- **MIDI** Files
- Image Mapping
- Java Scripts
- HTML Guestbooks
- Counters

### IT'S TIME TO POST YOUR WEB PAGE
After you've created a web page, you need to post it. To do this, you need a server that will host your web page. Many United Methodist churches have taken advantage of the

**MIDI:**
Musical Instrument Digital Interface. MIDI is a standardized format enabling synthesizers and computers to communicate. This allows musicians to compose music on a keyboard or digital piano and save the music information on the computer. MIDI files will have the extension ".mid" (for example, "amazgrac.mid"). MIDI files can be included in your HTML to allow music to be heard while people view your web page.

**.MID:**

Sound file extensions. A .mid (MIDI) file is generally background music created with a digital instrument such as a keyboard.

**.WAV:**

Sound file extensions. .Wav files can be any sound recorded through your PC's microphone. These are often spoken messages.

General Board of Global Ministries' offer for free web space.

*Location: http://gbgm-umc.org/docs/freeweb.html*

There are other Christian sites that provide free web space (generally in exchange for advertising). There are also web page hosting services that charge a fee. In some cases your ISP may provide you with a certain amount of web space as part of your monthly package. *America Online,* for example, provides 2MB of web space with each user name (you can have up to five user names on one account). By linking across user names, you actually can have up to 10MB for your web site through *America Online.*

Because *America Online* is so widely used, it is worth taking a moment to explain their process for posting a web page. Here's what you do:

1. Go to Keyword "My Place."
2. Click on "Go to My Place."
3. Click on "Upload."
4. Type in file name to be loaded.
5. Click "Select File."
6. Scroll through the directory to find the file to be uploaded. (This will be easier if you put all the files to be uploaded on one floppy disk.)
7. Click "Send."
8. Repeat steps 3 through 7 for additional files.

Don't forget that you need to upload not only your HTM files but also your GIF or JPG files, as well as any **.mid** or **.wav** files you have referenced in the source document.

The approach you take to posting your web page will depend on what hosting services are available to you and how big your plans are. For most churches the free 5–10MB of space is more than sufficient. If you want to include lots of video clips, sound files, and graphics, you may have to go to a professional web hosting service. These services can provide virtually unlimited space, generally starting at

$20–$30 per month for the first 20–40MB. Beyond that you pay as you grow. (If you have a church web site that requires more than 40MB, please e-mail me; I would like to see it! My e-mail address is Stmattumc@aol.com.

### DON'T FORGET TO PROMOTE YOURSELF!

Once you've posted your web page, you need to let people know that it's there. There are a variety of ways to do this, including the following:

**Search Engines.** You will want to register your web page on as many search engines as you can. Search engines are the "yellow pages" of the Internet. People who don't know where to look for a site often turn to a search engine for help. It goes without saying that if you are not included on that search engine, people may not find your web page. Generally, it doesn't cost anything to be included on the search engine; however, there is always some kind of application form to fill out—one for each search engine. This can be time-consuming, but it's very important. On page 89 you will find a listing of the major search engines to give you a start on this process.

It is possible to hire a service to do the work for you. For a fee, these services will list your web site with anywhere from one to two hundred different search engines. But the cost for this service can run over $100. The least expensive such service I have found thus far is *Register It* at ***www.register-it.com.*** They charge a flat rate of $39.99, with unlimited updates for a year. If you can afford it, you may find saving the time and effort worth the money. I haven't used any of these services myself, so I cannot attest to their effectiveness.

**Other Marketing Outlets**. It's good practice to include your web page in all other marketing you do. Here are a few places your URL ought to be seen:

- newspaper press releases (along with your church's phone number and address)
- posters for church events
- business cards
- church newsletter (on the masthead or beneath the return address)
- weekly church announcement page
- any other printed media

The more places your URL is seen, the more likely it is that people eventually will begin checking out your web page.

**Banner Services.** Banners are essentially what fund the Internet. Many businesses pay big money to have their banner appear in places most likely to be seen by potential customers. Most churches cannot afford banner space, but some Christian banner exchange programs will allow your church's banner to be seen on other web sites in exchange for banner space on your site. Unless you have something on your web page that would be of interest nationwide, this service may not be of much value to you. On the other hand, it is free and will probably increase the number of people who visit your site.

Now that we've covered the basics of getting a web page designed and posted, we are off to do some Web surfing of our own. We will begin by exploring in Chapter Five some of what is available that is specifically related to United Methodism; then, in Chapter Six, we will move on to other online Christian resources.

# *United Methodism in Cyberspace:*

# Web Sites You Can Really Use

Now that you've discovered what the Internet is about and how you might use it, it's time to have some fun. So wax up your board—we're going surfing. It is estimated that there are more than 50 million web pages posted worldwide. In the next two chapters we are going to review a few of them. Once you get started, you will discover many other interesting sites. See the Appendix on pages 94–96 for a list of more cool places on the Internet to surf.

In this chapter we will focus our attention on a few web sites of interest to United Methodists. Then in the following chapter we will expand our search to include a number of interesting non-United Methodist web sites. To make this chapter as helpful and useful as possible, I chose web sites that could provide United Methodist churches and pastors with practical tools to improve their communication and resourcing skills. (See Chapters Two and Three.)

Let's begin our tour by taking a look at some of the denominational resources at the general church level. Each site is listed by title and URL. Each site includes a paragraph describing the most helpful and most useful features of the site.

Generally speaking, these denominational web sites can help in several ways: First, they introduce you to the wide array of media resources available to you and your church. This includes books, curriculum resources, audio and video resources, computer software, and more. Second, they can help connect you to the human resources available at the district, conference, and general church levels. Many of the sites include downloadable information related to United Methodism, such as denominational history, doctrine, and social standards. They also provide information related to the wider mission and ministry of our denomination. Third, some sites can be a source of current (and archived) news and information of interest to United Methodists.

You can use some of the information and resources you find on these sites immediately; others you will want to file away mentally until a specific need arises. For example, suppose your church is preparing to start a new ministry, such as daycare. It would be wise to do a demographic study of your community. To do this you could go to the General Board of Global Ministries home page and order a demographic study—right over the Internet! When you get your study, if you have questions, you will find a phone number and e-mail address right on the web page.

Take another example: Suppose your firstborn is going off to college, and you want to know if there is a United Methodist campus ministry on the college campus. You could find this information on the "Campus Ministry" page of the General Board of Higher Education and Ministry's web site. A final example: You are moving to a new community, and you are looking for a United Methodist church near your home. It is likely that you'll find the information you are looking for on the home page of "United Methodist Information—the Official United Methodist Home Page." In fact, the church near your home may even have a web page—thousands now do—where you can find the times of worship, information about the church's ministries, and maybe even a map to the church.

These are just a few of the ways in which the web sites listed in this chapter may provide you with practical help. As you read along, I'm sure you'll find more uses for these sites!

### WEB SITES AT THE GENERAL CHURCH LEVEL

You most likely will want to use the following web sites for reference purposes. These web sites should contain most of the information you need about ministries offered through the church's general agencies. In many cases, you can contact agency staff directly via e-mail. In earlier chapters we talked about how the Internet can provide resources for you and your church, as well as offer valuable opportunities for communication. Browse these sites to begin to experience these benefits.

### *United Methodist Information—The Official Website of The United Methodist Church*

Coordinated and maintained by United Methodist Communications, this web site is a great starting point for United Methodist churches. One thing you will find at this site is a directory to the more than 2,400 United Methodist churches with web pages. The directory is organized by state, allowing you immediate access to churches all across the country. Checking out random web pages from across the denomination is a great way to exchange ideas for mission and ministry. Most pages include e-mail links that allow you to communicate directly with the church to discuss ideas that interest you.

This site also includes links to denominational news and events, recent judicial council decisions, employment opportunities, and much more. The "People Connecting" link provides access (by telephone, e-mail, and Fax) to United Methodist agencies, conference offices, bishops, and foundations. It also provides access to international links.

Other links from the "United Methodist Information" site include information on apportionment money at work, mission and ministry, schools and scholarships, and publications. Under the link "About United Methodism" is a wealth of information that would be especially helpful in introducing new members to the denomination. Links include United Methodist history, doctrine, discipline, organizational structure, worship and sacraments, and worldwide mission and ministry.

*Location: http://www.umc.org*

### *General Board of Church and Society, The United Methodist Church*

This valuable web site explains the work of this general agency, issue advocacy, the Social Principles, and more. The "Action Alerts" link helps keep Christians apprised of pending government legislation. The site also contains a link to senators and representatives, including both telephone numbers and e-mail addresses. The "Christian Social Action" link allows access to an online version of the printed publication with the same name. The online version includes articles from the current issue, as well as from past issues. You can subscribe online and even e-mail your personal suggestions for topics to be addressed in upcoming issues. There are also links to the United Nations. Under the "Resource" section of this web site, visitors will find "Word from Washington," the

*Environmental Justice* newsletter, "Immigration Updates," the *Peace with Justice* newsletter, and a listing of printed resources related to political action. These resources will help keep you and your church up-to-date on any number of social concerns.
*Location: http://www.umc-gbcs.org*

### General Board of Discipleship

This web site provides articles, printed resources, information about training events, and a connection to staff at the General Board of Discipleship to assist in virtually any area of Christian discipleship in the local church. An online bookstore for Discipleship Resources *(http://www.discipleshipresources.org/)* is also a part of the site.

This web site has three main divisions: "Discipleship Ministries," "Quest," and "The Upper Room." In the "Discipleship Ministries" division you will discover an extensive list of links related to the various areas of ministry represented by this board, such as ministry with children, youth, adults, families; Christian education; camping; ethnic local church concerns; evangelism; small-group ministries; and many more.

The "Evangelism" page includes information on Vision 2000, Offering Christ Today schools, the Lay Witness Mission program, and an online version of the *Offering Christ Today* newsletter. The "Faith-Sharing" link offers printed resources and information about training events to equip you and your congregation to share the gospel.

The "Christian Education" page includes resources, articles, and information about training events to support Christian education in the local church. The "Stewardship" page includes information on Growing Giving seminars, Planned Giving, and a large number of articles on Christian giving. The "Adult Ministries" page features articles, comments, links, information about training events, and resources about single adults, younger, middle, and older adults. The "Ethnic Local Church Concerns" page provides information about and applications for grants available for Ethnic Local Church Concerns programs or projects.

The "Quest" division of the web site invites churches to consider a new way of thinking about what it means to be the church. It seeks to improve a congregation's effectiveness in mission and ministry by building relationships, knowledge, and leadership. By offering resources, events, staff support, and a leadership network, the "Quest" page helps local churches develop and refine many areas of ministry. *Location: http://www.gbod.org*

### The Upper Room

The Upper Room is included under the General Board of Discipleship's web site, but it contains such a wealth of information that it merits separate mention. "The Upper Room" home page includes a variety of links to help Christians progress in their faith journeys. There is a daily devotional that corresponds to the popular *Upper Room* magazine, along with an archive of previous devotions. There is also information about *Devo'Zine,* a devotional magazine for youth. The web site includes links to *Alive Now* and *Pockets* magazines, and it has an online bookstore. You'll also find valuable information about the Upper Room's Healing and Wholeness Ministries, the Walk to Emmaus program, the Crysalis program (for youth), and other resources for personal spiritual growth. *Location: http://www.upperroom.org*

### General Board of Global Ministries, United Methodist Church

This is a web site you will want to bookmark for two reasons: The first reason is that this site boasts a great deal of information related to the mission and ministry of United Methodists across our nation and world. To use this site effectively, you will need to do one of two things: (1) Click on "Search," and then type in a key word related to the information for which you are searching. (2) Use the drop-down menu near the bottom of the page and look through the alphabetical listing for the topic you need. For example, suppose you want to find out what The United Methodist Church is doing to assist flood victims, and how your church can be involved. You could type the word *flood* in the search box, or you could scroll down to "1998 Storms and Floods" in the drop-down menu. This site also offers excellent information about ideas or opportunities related to AIDS ministries, world hunger, the Advance, and a number of other areas of ministry.

The second reason to bookmark this web site is because it provides free web space for United Methodist churches and organizations. More than two thousand local churches, districts, annual conferences, and jurisdictional and general agencies are hosted by the General Board of Global Ministries' server. GBGM also provides web space for United Methodist Women's groups at all levels, whether local, district, national, or global. It provides up to 5MB of free web space, and the GBGM web page includes all the detail you need to get online with them.
*Location: http://gbgm-umc.org*

### General Board of Higher Education and Ministry

This site includes the divisions of "Ordained Ministry" and "Higher Education." The "Ordained Ministry" division offers sections aimed specifically at chaplaincy, local pastors and elders, deacons and diaconal ministers. Information on the orders of ordained ministry can be found on this site, along with a report entitled "Agenda 21." This project, initiated by the Association of United Methodist

Theological Schools, looks at whether the theological schools are serving the church in the most faithful and effective way. People involved in the work of conference boards of ordained ministry may be delighted to know that the complete *Board of Ordained Ministry Handbook* for 1996-2000 is included on this site. For those seeking information about the process of candidacy, the course of study, ordination, and even retirement planning, this online handbook is a helpful resource.

The "Higher Education" division of this site offers links to United Methodist-related schools, colleges, universities, and theological schools. There is also information about United Methodist loan and scholarship programs. There are also links to campus ministries.

*Location: http://www.gbhem.org*

### OTHER WEB SITES AT THE NATIONAL LEVEL

The web sites in this section go beyond the specific parameters of the general agencies and commissions; they address in detail specific areas of ministry or provide other information applicable to United Methodists nationwide.

### Bishops by Jurisdictions

This site, which is maintained by InfoServ, lists United Methodist bishops by jurisdiction. Bishops' names, addresses, telephone and fax numbers, and e-mail addresses (if available) are included.

*Location: http://www.umc.org/jurisconf/bishops.html*

### United Methodist Information: UM News Service

This site provides "headlines" from news stories produced by the United Methodist News Service, the official news agency of The United Methodist Church. The nice thing about this site is that it grants anyone hitting the site permission to use

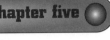
the releases and the accompanying photographs, when available. The site does request that credit be given to United Methodist News Service. Those hitting the site may cut and paste news articles (and digitized photos) directly into a church newsletter or other publication. With the expansive news archive included, this site would be cumbersome to use were it not for the built-in search engine. To find news articles related to a particular subject or event, a visitor simply goes to "Search" and enters a key word.
*Location: http://www.umc.org/umns*

### United Methodist Reporter Interactive

To find the latest religion-related news from the pages of the *United Methodist Reporter* and *National Christian Reporter,* click on "News" and begin with the "HotTopics" link on this site. This web page is updated each week, with dozens of articles taken from the pages of these two publications. The "SoulFood" link includes a variety of inspirational stories, a collection of Lectionary readings, and a "History of Hymns" section.
*Location: http://www.umr.org*

### United Methodist Committee on Relief

This page keeps visitors updated about important relief efforts throughout the world. It includes links to UMCOR's three emphases: emergency response, world hunger and poverty, and refugees. This site offers specific ways that you or your church can help when disaster strikes. For the most up-to-date information about specific UMCOR responses to emergency needs, click on "Emergency Response," then on the "UMCOR Hotline" link.
*Location: http://gbgm-umc.org/units/umcor*

### Unofficial United Methodist Church Page

Maintained by David Mullens, this page has become a fixture of United Methodism on the Internet. It is well-maintained, and it has a wealth

**ADOBE ACROBAT:**

Adobe Acrobat is a program that allows you to download a document in its exact graphic design. To view an Adobe file you must have the matching software, which you can download for free from the Adobe web site. (http://www.adobe.com)

of resources. A drop-down menu of links connects you to virtually all things Methodist. There are also links to international Methodist resources and information. This site supports a chat room, where you can connect to others on a more personal level. Another nice feature (especially if you happen to be looking for ministry-related employment) is the "Jobs Page." This Christian ministry help-wanted page is provided free of charge by "Unofficial United Methodist Church Page." If your church has a position to be filled, you can post it on this page.

*Location:* ***http://www.netins.net/showcase/umsource***

### List of Annual Conference Offices

A listing of annual conference web sites is found at the site address provided below. Not all conferences have a web page; and for the most part, the annual conference pages are not among the best on the Web. Many of them resemble the online version of the conference journal: reports, addresses, and a greeting from the bishop. However, a few have attractive, creative designs and rapid download times, as well as a few extras such as scrolls, music, **Adobe Acrobat** files, even video clips. Some are designed for unchurched visitors. Some include services to help people find a local church; others have kids' stuff or devotionals.

I really don't want to choose a "best conference page," but some of the conference sites I really like are Missouri West, West Ohio, Minnesota, Kansas East, Holston, California Pacific, and of course, New England.

*Location:* ***http://www.umc.org/offices.html***

### WEB SITES AT THE LOCAL CHURCH LEVEL

I selected a few local church web sites for a couple of reasons: First, the quality of the design of some of these pages makes them excellent resources as you design your own church's page. Many are award-winning and well worth studying as you prepare your own web page. Second, despite the average quality of design of some of the other sites I've mentioned here, I chose those sites because the ministries they feature are noteworthy or well-known. Often these pages have ministry ideas that can be shared. You can contact these churches directly by e-mail.

### UMC ONE

The web site of First United Methodist Church in Myrtle Beach, South Carolina, is one of the pioneer church web sites on the Internet. It was originally one of the largest link pages on the Internet devoted to United Methodism. It provides host space to other ministries. It has now evolved into an online ministry and has a design worth studying.
*Location: http://www.umc1.org*

### Ashton United Methodist Church

This award-winning web page is a strong example of web design. Note the use of real audio clips and links of local interest to draw the unchurched.
*Location:*
*http://members.aol.com/ashtonumc/index.html*

### First United Methodist Church, Orlando, Florida

This award-winning site boasts a very attractive frame-enhanced web page. Note the inclusion of a membership e-mail directory. What a great idea to enhance communication!
*Location: http://www.magicnet.net/fumco/fumco.html*

### St. Matthews United Methodist Church

This site uses pull-down menus to save space, and a photo gallery paints a picture of ministry. The site also includes separate pages specifically for children and youth.
*Location: http://www.stmattumc.org*

### Ginghamsburg Church

This is one of the fastest-growing churches in The United Methodist Church. The web site, which is a good example of web design, show-cases some of Ginghamsburg's ministries.
*Location: http://www.ginghamsburg.org*

### Glide Memorial United Methodist Church

This page tells an exciting story of ministry. This growing church is an excellent example of community-based ministry. It provides more than a million meals each year, along with healthcare, job training, parenting classes, substance abuse programs, and much more.
*Location: http://www.glide.org*

### Highland Park United Methodist Church

This church has 11,000 members, and it continues to grow. This particular page makes extensive use of *Adobe Acrobat*. It also provides the *E-pistles*, an e-mail-based devotional.
*Location: http://www.hpumc.org*

## RESOURCES FOR CONGREGATIONAL DEVELOPMENT

The Web offers much help for leaders involved in areas of church growth, congrega-tional development or transformation, or new church development. The following web sites list resources for congregational development.

## Transformation

The web sites below can help facil-itate positive change in the life and ministry of any local church.

### General Board of Global Ministries Office of Research

If it is your desire to transform the ministry of your church to better meet the needs of

the community you serve, the place to begin is with a demographic study. For $216 you can have an accurate, detailed accounting of the residents of your community and what they say their needs are.
*Location: http://gbgm-umc.org/research/index.html*

### 21st Century Strategies, Inc.

This home page of Bill Easum looks at the church and its possibilities for growth in the twenty-first century. It features lots of resources, consultant services, church planting resources, networking, training events, and more.
*Location: http://www.easum.com*

### New Church Development

If you're considering developing a new church, it might be helpful to communicate with others who have gone before you. The web sites below provide useful information about new church starts and some ideas for new church development.

### Dove of the Desert United Methodist Church

This new congregation in Glendale, Arizona, has pioneered the concept of multiple worship services. They have grown to more than 700 in worship attendance, offering three distinctly different worship services. Traditional, contemporary, and Generation X worship all take place under the same roof at different times, allowing the church to reach a broader community.
*Location: http://www.desertsw.org/dove*

### 21st Century Strategies, Inc.: "The Easum Report"

Bill Easum has consulted with hundreds of congregations throughout the United States to assist them in both transformation and new church development. On this web site, he offers some helpful insights for those approaching a new church start.
*Location: http://www.easum.com/church.htm*

71

### New Congregational Development, General Board of Discipleship

This site includes recommended resources and announcements about training events.
*Location: http://www.gbod.org/evangelism/programs /congregation/default.html*

## Spiritual Growth

There are excellent books and magazines to help congregations transform their ministries, and there are a number of web sites dedicated to personal spiritual growth. The United Methodist-sponsored sites below are dedicated to the spiritual growth of individual believers.

### The Center for Spiritual Formation

This site is affiliated with the Central Pennsylvania Conference of The United Methodist Church. It offers training in spiritual development, retreats, and special events.
*Location:*
*http://www.cpcumc.org/spiritual/spiritual.htm*

### The Academy for Spiritual Formation

This academy is a disciplined Christian community that emphasizes a holistic spirituality that nurtures body, mind, and spirit. Each academy takes two years to complete. Participants meet in residence at a specified location for eight five-day sessions over a two-year period. Less-intensive five-day academies are also available.
*Location:*
*http://www.upperroom.org/resources/academy.html*

## History and Theology Resources

The Internet is particularly well-suited for sharing historical and theological resources. You will find not only online versions of some of the great historical and theological works but also ample

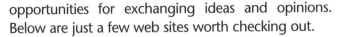

opportunities for exchanging ideas and opinions. Below are just a few web sites worth checking out.

### The Wesleys and Their Times

This site hosts a collection of Wesleyan resources put together by the General Board of Global Ministries. Among the resources available are a collection of high-quality scanned historic Methodist images that you may download. A collection of Charles Wesley's hymns (words and MIDI music) is also available, along with a tremendous collection of John Wesley's writings.
*Location:* **http://gbgm-umc.org/umhistory/wesley**

### Sermons on Several Occasions by John Wesley

This site is maintained by the Wesley Center for Applied Theology. Sermons are indexed by both title and number. The site also includes Wesley's preface to each of five sermon series.
*Location:*
**http://www.netins.net/showcase/umsource/1872.html**

### Good News

Good News is an influential evangelical renewal movement within The United Methodist Church. This site provides encouragement and resources for evangelical witness within The United Methodist Church. Visitors to this site can review articles from current or previous issues of the printed publication.
*Location:* **http://www.goodnewsmag.org**

### The Cross and Flame Logo

This web page includes valuable information about the history and meaning of the logo of The United Methodist Church.
*Location:* **http://www.umc.org/about/4cros.html**

### HymnSite.Com

This site contains a large selection of MIDI (digitally recorded) hymns from *The United*

*Methodist Hymnal*—all in the public domain. You are encouraged to download, use, and enjoy any of the music that you find here. If you would like to add background music to your web page, this is a great place to look.

*Location: http://www.hymnsite.com*

### Evangelism

The following United Methodist-related sites on evangelism are worth a look.

### Frazer UMC

This page from Frazer Memorial's site includes Frazer's comprehensive evangelism plan.

*Location:*

*http://www.mindspring.com/~frazerum/evnglism.htm*

### General Board of Discipleship Evangelism Home Page

This page provides resources, programs, and events that are designed to help congregations tell the good news of Jesus Christ and live out their primary task of reaching out to others, receiving and nurturing them, and sending them out in ministry in the world.

*Location: http://www.gbod.org/evangelism/default.html*

### The Foundation for Evangelism

This well-designed web page includes resources, news items, articles, and links related to evangelism. There is also an online version of *Forward* magazine, information on the E. Stanley Jones Professorships of Evangelism, and a virtual walking tour of the foundation.

*Location: http://www.evangelize.org*

### Missions

Lots of information about United Methodists in mission is available on the Internet. The following are just a few sites to get you started.

74

### United Methodists in Mission

This site is a General Board of Global Ministries-sponsored link list of United Methodists in mission. It includes paid and volunteer mission opportunities, mission alerts, and much more.

*Location: http://gbgm-umc.org/mission*

### Appalachia Service Project

This site provides much helpful information for those preparing to take a mission trip to the Appalachia Service Project.

*Location: http://www.asphome.org*

### Red Bird Mission

Red Bird Mission is well-known for its work camp experience.

*Location: http://hwmin.gbgm-umc.org/conferences /redbirdmission*

### <u>Worship</u>

The following web sites deal with worship and worship preparation, and are sponsored by United Methodists.

### General Board of Discipleship Worship Home Page

This site provides a worship discussion room, relevant articles, and seasonal resources for worship.

*Location: http://www.gbod.org/worship/default.html*

### The Fellowship of United Methodists in Music and Worship Arts

This site provides information on membership in "The Fellowship" and on contact persons within the organization. It also provides information about the biennial national convocation.

*Location:*
*http://members.aol.com/fummwa/fummwa.htm*

### The Order of Saint Luke Home Page

The Order of Saint Luke is a dispersed community of women and men (lay and clergy) from different denominations who seek to live the sacramental life. This web site contains information on membership and publication.

*Location: http://www.Saint-Luke.org*

## Devotions From United Methodists

There are literally hundreds of online devotionals available. The following are just a few examples.

### The Upper Room Daily Devotional

This site includes the daily devotional from the *Upper Room* magazine, as well as a link to archived devotions.

*Location:*
*http://www.upperroom.org/devotional/default.html*

### E-pistles World Wide Web Home Page

This is the home page of an e-mail-based weekly devotional. Simply sign up; each Monday morning, you will receive the weekly devotional from the Rev. Eric Folkerth of Highland Park United Methodist Church in Dallas, Texas. There are more than 1,000 subscribers in 35 states and 11 foreign countries; the service is free.

*Location: http://www.hpumc.org/ehome.html*

### Daily Devotions: A Few Moments With God

This is a daily devotional from Rev. Ronald Newhouse of the First United Methodist Church in Red Oak, Texas.

*Location:*
*http://www.dallas.net/~ronnew/devotions.htm*

### JUST FOR FUN

Sometimes when you are surfing the Internet, you will come across things that are fun, interesting, or unusual. Here's one of my favorite "just for fun" sites.

### Hotel Viktoria

Would you believe that The United Methodist Church owns a hotel in the Swiss Alps? (I'm hoping that they will give me free lodging in exchange for this shameless plug!) One could definitely feel close to God here.

*Location: http://www.viktoria.ch*

### NEED MORE LINKS?

After reading through this chapter and checking out the sites, if there is still something you haven't found related to Methodism, here are a couple of places to consider.

### BethlehemLinks

Sponsored by Bethlehem United Methodist Church, Thornton, Pennsylvania, this site offers an extensive, well-organized collection of links. As you look for links to include in your church's web page, this is a great place to start.

*Location: http://www.bethlehemlinks.org/frames.htm*

### Pastor's Pointers Graphics-Rich United Methodist Links Page

This is another fairly comprehensive United Methodist link page, which is supported by the Minnesota Annual Conference. It contains hundreds of United Methodist-related links.

*Location: http://www.mumac.org/pp.html*

# *Meeting Christians in Cyberspace:*

# Other Christian Web Sites You Can Use

In the previous chapter we surfed the Internet for United Methodist-related web sites. In this chapter, we widen our search to include other Christian web sites.

This can be overwhelming, since the volume of Christian resources on the Internet is almost beyond imagination. But you've got to start somewhere, so this chapter lists a few sites from a variety of areas of Christian ministry. From there you can do your own investigating to find the sites that best meet you and your church's needs and interests. Again, don't forget the Appendix on pages 94–96 for a list of other cool places to go.

### CARE TO SEE SOME MEGA SITES?

The following web sites are among the largest Christian sites on the Internet. Each has its strengths; but combined, they provide you with resources related to virtually every area of Christian ministry. They feature well-organized link sections, biblical study resources, tools for evangelism, and much more. Some of them even provide web space for local churches or parachurch ministries.

### Goshen Net

This all-purpose Christian resource page is one of the finest on the Internet. It includes hundreds of links on everything from audio-visual equipment for worship to Christian television and radio stations. If you're not sure where to look, this is a great place to start. The site includes Bible study resources, Christian news, Christian shareware, classified ads, Web development tools, and a whole lot more.

*Location: http://www.goshen.net*

### Net Ministries Home Page

Aside from an excellent assortment of links and resources, the "Net Ministries Home Page" provides free web hosting services for churches, Christian ministries, and some non-profit organizations. You can also submit your link to be included in their list of churches. This is another major site that you will want to bookmark.

*Location: http://netministries.org*

### Gospel Communications Network

This site hosts a tremendous selection of resources, and it includes a built-in search engine to help you find your way around. GCN is host to some of the better-known Christian resources on the Internet. Go to the drop-down list of member ministries and scroll through it. You'll find the "American Tract Society," "Billy Graham Training Center," "Fellowship of Christian Athletes," "InterVarsity Press," "Luis Palau Evangelistic Association," "The Navigators," and "Youth Specialties," to name a few. You'll want to bookmark this site.

*Location: http://www.gospelcom.net*

79

## Resources for Growing Your Church/Evangelism

The following are resources to help you and your congregation fulfill Christ's commission to make disciples (Matthew 28:19-20).

### 21st Century Strategies, Inc.

This site, hosted by Bill Easum, is an excellent resource for those seeking tools for evangelism. (See page 71 for a description of this site.)
*Location: **http://www.easum.com***

### Christian Internet Ministries Home Page

This site, dedicated to sharing the good news of Christ with the Internet community, is essentially a "cyber church." Through prayer requests, praise reports, teaching, and more, this site is pioneering "cyber evangelism," perhaps in the same way that the first radio and television evangelists did.
*Location: **http://www.cyber-church.org/Home.htm***

## Bible Study

The following are some of the excellent sites on the Internet for engaging in Bible study and for teaching.

### Biblical Studies Foundation

This very popular biblical studies page is likely to have half a million hits a year. While focusing on biblical studies, it includes links to a variety of other areas of Christian life and ministry. For those new to the site, it also includes a short list of the six to eight most popular pages on the site.
*Location: **http://www.bible.org***

### Bible 101

This page features Internet sites for people interested in studying classic religious works, theology, texts of the Bible, and Bible studies (including original language studies), reference works, and

much more. This site also includes a biblical and theological index. This site is very comprehensive, with
excellent study tools for in-depth Bible study.
*Location: http://www.bible101.org/main.html*

### Walking Thru the Bible

This site hosts a series of Bible class
lessons and sermon outlines to help you go through
the Bible in one year. The series can be viewed on-
screen and/or printed. The entire Old Testament and
New Testament series are available in files formatted in
WordPerfect for easy downloading. This site is a valuable resource to anyone who wants to teach through
the Bible in worship or in a weekly study.
*Location: http://fly.hiwaay.net/~wgann/walk.htm*

### World Wide Study Bible

This is an excellent site to help
with Bible study or sermon preparation. You choose
the biblical chapter and verses, and the site supplies
the executable outline, commentary—even complete
classic sermons on the passage you selected! The site
also includes several translations of the Bible, an online
concordance, a Bible dictionary, and much more. I use
this site virtually every week.
*Location: http://ccel.wheaton.edu/wwsb*

### Sermon Preparation

For pastors or lay preachers who
must prepare a sermon week after week, the Internet
is a gift from God. There is a tremendous selection of
complete sermons, outlines, illustrations, and other
helps for sermon preparation. Visit the following web
sites as a way to get started.

### Kir-Shalom Internet Ministry

This web page has dozens of links
to sermons that are based on the Revised Common
Lectionary. After you scroll through this extensive list,
you come to the Lectionary-based sermons of the Rev.

Richard J. Fairchild. The page also includes links to sermon illustrations, sermons not based on the Lectionary, series of sermons, and more.
*Location: **http://www.rockies.net/~spirit***

### Desperate Preacher's Site

If the words "sermon block" mean anything to you, bookmark this site! The heart of this site is the Scripture forum: Here visitors can click on upcoming Lectionary texts and share their thoughts regarding the Scripture readings for a particular Sunday. They also can read what others have said about the readings. It is a great way to get the creative process flowing. The site also includes complete sermons, children's sermons, and a variety of sermon preparation helps.
*Location: **http://www.javacasa.com/dps***

## Worship Resources

Besides helping with sermon preparation, a number of web sites feature excellent resources for helping prepare the whole worship experience. Pastors, music directors, and others involved in leading worship will find some helpful ideas here.

### The Institute for Worship Studies

This site provides training for pastors, music ministers, church leaders, and laypeople, and provides resources for worship education and renewal.
*Location: **http://members.aol.com/worshipweb***

### Worship Works

This site supports a subscription service with resources for worship leaders and planners. While you must be a subscriber to take full advantage of the site, it does include a free issue of *Worship Works* and a handful of worship-related links.
*Location: **http://www.worshipworks.org***

### DramaShare

This site promotes drama for worship and evangelism. It includes downloadable scripts.
*Location: http://www3.sk.sympatico.ca/dramashr*

### Worship Resource Center

This site provides resources and multiple links for worship preparation.
*Location: http://praise.net/worship*

### Christian Copyright Licensing International

This site can help you understand copyright law as it applies to reproduction of music in the church, and it can assist you in obtaining a CCLI license. It also provides a variety of helpful worship resources.
*Location: http://www.ccli.com*

### Lift Up Your Hearts Home Page

This site, which is sponsored by the Evangelical Lutheran Church in Canada, features an impressive selection of resources for worship and spiritual growth, as well as an excellent set of links.
*Location: http://www.golden.net/worship*

### Youth Ministry

I rarely meet anyone involved in youth ministry who does not readily welcome new ideas and resources. The following are several web sites that might provide you with some new ideas and resources, as well as links to other sites.

### Christian Youth Resources

This recently updated site includes connections to sites about magazines, music, devotions, drama, and more, all related to Christian youth ministry.
*Location: http://www.milkandhoney.ab.ca/cyr*

### General Board of Discipleship Youth Ministry

This site includes articles and resource listings of interest to youth workers. It also includes a discussion room.

Location: *http://www.gbod.org/youth/default.html*

### Youth Specialties

You may want to bookmark this site. "Youth Specialties" is one of the leading suppliers of resources and training for youth ministries.

Location: *http://www.gospelcom.net/ys*

### Group's Youth Ministry

This site features a nice collection of youth ministry resources from the publishers of *Group Magazine*. The site includes ideas for retreats, training events, work camps, and much more.

Location: *http://www.grouppublishing.com/youth*

### E-ZINES

"E-zines" refer to online magazines; many magazines now have online versions. Some of them restrict access to subscribers only, but many others offer free access. Check these out:

### CCM Online

This is the online version of *CCM* magazine, covering the world of contemporary Christian music. The site includes interviews with top Christian recording artists, tour dates, reviews, and much more related to the burgeoning world of contemporary Christian music. This is a particularly helpful resource for workers with youth, and for parents who want to get their kids turned on to Christian rock, rap, pop, funk—or whatever else they are into!

Location: *http://www.ccmcom.com*

### The Church Music Report

This online magazine provides a variety of helpful resources for church musicians and

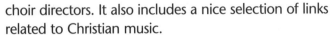

choir directors. It also includes a nice selection of links related to Christian music.
*Location: http://www.tcmr.com*

### PAGES FOR CHILDREN

If you are looking for some good places where your children can hang out on the Web, here are some excellent sites. They offer activities, games, stories, jokes, and a lot more.

### *MacGillicuddy's Home Page*

This site for older children includes activities, jokes, and a lot more. This page is a ministry of Greenville United Methodist Church in New York.
*Location: http://www.geocities.com/Heartland/5344*

### *Parenting the Next Generation*

This site is an educational resource provided by Alan and Hui Meng, members of Faith Methodist Church in Singapore. Stories for children are included on this site.
*Location:*
*http://www.geocities.com/Heartland/Ranch/2200*

### *Pockets Magazine*

Visit this site, and you'll find lots of things for kids, such as a daily devotional, jokes, poems, and games. There is also a section for adults, with a family litany, articles about children's spirituality, and information about how to use *Pockets* with children.
*Location: http://www.upperroom.org/pockets*

### DEVOTIONALS ONLINE

A number of well-prepared devotionals are available on the Internet from a wide variety of sources. Here are just a few web sites to check out.

### *Guideposts*

Every day this site features a new devotional that includes a personal spiritual experi-

ence from a favorite *Daily Guideposts* author; a specially selected Bible verse; and a thoughtful prayer.
*Location: http://www.guideposts.org/daily/daily.shtml*

### GCN's Daily & Weekly Devotionals

Gospel Communications Network hosts a number of excellent devotional sites, including: "Our Daily Bread Devotional," "The NIV Quiet Time Bible," "Campus Journal Devotional," "Oswald Chambers' *My Utmost for His Highest*," and others. If you are looking for a daily or weekly devotional, this page includes links to some of the most popular devotional sites on the Web.
*Location: http://www.gospelcom.net/devo*

### Journey of Faith

This site features a daily devotional that takes you through the Bible in one year. It includes an archive that allows you to catch up on any devotional you may have missed.
*Location: http://www.crusade.org/cgi/journey.cgi*

### CHURCH GROWTH

The following sites feature several well-known resources, authors, and consultants in the area of church growth. All these web pages are expansive and well-designed.

### Net Results

This site is an online extension of Herb Miller's *Net Results* publication. Like the publication, the web page is dedicated to gathering and sharing effective ideas for church growth and development. The page also includes information about upcoming workshops and local church consultations, national events, and much more. If you are looking for practical, applicable ideas to strengthen the ministry of your local church and to help it grow, this is a good place to start.
*Location: http://www.llano.net/net-results*

### The Lyle Schaller Page

For the past thirty-four years, Lyle Schaller has served as a parish consultant to approximately 5,000 congregations from sixty religious traditions. This site is well worth your time.

*Location: http://www.leadnet.org/d5bschallerpg.html*

### Spirit Venture Ministries

*Spirit Venture Ministries* is an inter-denominational nonprofit organization, established in 1994 to serve as a base for the ministry of Dr. Leonard I. Sweet. Its goal is to develop and provide leadership resources. Leonard Sweet's ministry is probably best known for the publication of *Sweet's SoulCafe*. Check this site out.

*Location: http://www.leonardsweet.com*

### Percept

This site features one of the better-known national demographic services. It offers a service similar to the General Board of Global Ministries' demographic studies. I have used both; though "Percept" is an excellent resource, I have found the Global Ministries site to be a bit better and less expensive. However, "Percept" is widely used across denominational lines, and it is certainly worth looking into.

*Location: http://www.perceptnet.com*

## MEGA CHURCHES YOU CAN LEARN FROM

A handful of churches have experienced phenomenal growth and have become well-known. Many of these churches have web sites with resources that allow you to learn from their experiences. I have included a cross section of denominational and nondenominational church web sites.

### Willow Creek Community Church

Willow Creek's web page is much more than a church home page. The Willow Creek Association includes in-house publishing, drama, music, and other worship resources, as well as outstanding leadership conferences. Willow Creek sponsors a number of large training events, for which you can register online. Visitors also can hear real audio clips of Willow Creek music or can take a "Quick Time Virtual Reality Tour" of the 4,500-seat auditorium. Some of the most helpful information is found under the "Resources" link.

*Location: http://www.willownet.com*

### Saddleback Valley Community Church

Under the leadership of Rick Warren, this church is well-known as the "purpose-driven church." Like Willow Creek, Saddleback provides a variety of resources for church growth and ministry, including leadership seminars. One portion of the web page I found interesting was titled "Tech Land," explaining what goes on behind the scenes (audio-visually) to make worship and other ministries possible at Saddleback Church. If your ministry in the church involves audio, sound, and video equipment, you will find this site particularly interesting. You may also find yourself somewhat envious!

*Location: http://www.saddleback.com*

### First Baptist Church of Jacksonville, Florida

This downtown church is recognized as one of the largest and fastest-growing churches in the Southern Baptist Convention. It is under the shared leadership of Dr. Homer G. Lindsay, Jr., and Dr. Jerry Vines. This web page includes information about the church's ministry, as well as links to a bookstore, staff contacts, and other opportunities.

*Location: http://www.fbcjax.com*

### Community Church of Joy

The web page for this Glendale, Arizona, church provides prospective visitors with ample information about the ministries of the church. This site also includes links to the church's internation-

al leadership center and to Joy's Leadership Center.
*Location: **http://www.ccoj.com***

## DON'T FORGET THE SEARCH ENGINES

As you may recall, search engines are those indispensable tools that allow you to find whatever you're looking for among the millions of web pages out there. This chapter barely scratched the surface of Christian resources available on the Internet. If you're searching for something very specific, the place to begin is with a search engine.

Below are the URLs for a few of the larger search engines.

- *Infoseek*
*Location: **http://guide.infoseek.com***
- *Excite*
*Location: **http://www.excite.com***
- *Lycos*
*Location: **http://a2z.lycos.com***
- *Yahoo!*
*Location: **http://www.yahoo.com***
- *AltaVista*
*Location: **http://altavista.digital.com***
- *Magellan*
*Location: **http://www.mckinley.com***
- *WebCrawler*
*Location: **http://webcrawler.com***
- *HotBot*
*Location: **http://www.hotbot.com***

# The Church in Cyberspace: What's Ahead?

In many areas of life, a review of the past can help us predict the future. But the Internet has emerged so quickly that there is little basis upon which to make projections. With that in mind, I wouldn't want to say that the future of the Internet is certain. However, I do think some changes are coming—and some of those changes will have implications for how the church uses the technology that the Internet offers.

### CHANGE IS GOOD, RIGHT?

So, what are some of the changes we may be seeing in the years ahead? Here are a few of my educated guesses:

First, I think it would be safe to say that Internet access will continue to increase. When the telephone was first introduced, access was quite limited. But over time its use increased, and the telephone became a necessity. In a similar way, cable television was once limited to a small percentage of American homes. Broadcast networks laughed at the idea that anyone would pay to receive a television signal. Yet, today we see millions of homes boasting not only cable television but also satellite dishes—and now even direct satellite. I would not be surprised if a decade from now Internet access will be commonplace in most homes in the United States of America, as well as in other developed nations.

Second, Internet access is likely to become not only more widely available but also increasingly faster. Both cable television companies and telephone companies have the technology now to offer high-speed Internet access to individual homes. What is lacking is the infrastructure to support the technology. High-speed access is already available to homes in many metropolitan areas, but it could take several years before such access reaches the more remote areas of our country. Remember how access to cable television took several years to become readily available?

Third, another trend that will probably increase is the use of the Internet for educational and business purposes. The Internet makes information and educational resources equally accessible anywhere people are able to get online. In many areas of the United States, home schooling is increasing at a dramatic rate. It is possible that the Internet will contribute to the continued growth of home schooling.

The Internet also makes it possible for an increasing number of people to work at home. Telecommuting could free up precious office space, reduce traffic in the urban areas, and, I believe, increase productivity. However, what will also increase as a result of this trend is the potential for people to work and live in isolation from one another.

## BUT WHAT ARE THE "NET" RESULTS FOR THE CHURCH?

What do all these changes mean for the church's life and ministry? Increased Internet access means that electronic communication will become more and more a part of everyday life. Churches that haven't learned to use these tools by the turn of the century will be considered antiquated. (Perhaps as antiquated as the United Methodist churches that entered this decade without indoor plumbing!)

The increase in the speed of the Internet opens up some exciting possibilities for the church. Greater speed allows web sites to be more interactive and to make greater use of multimedia. This is great news for churches that want to present themselves effectively on the Web. Many businesses can get away with a static, catalog-style web page to display their wares. But the church is a living and dynamic thing; it expresses itself with activity, movement, song, and dance. So here's the good news: Web pages of the near future will be able to include audio/video clips of entire choir anthems, praise choruses, or even sermons. People with limited ability to leave home or people separated from the congregation by physical distance will be able to participate in real-time interactive Bible study wherever they are. Educational events, seminars, and meetings can be brought to our homes, making us better stewards of time and resources.

All this brings us to the concern about isolation. Some people anticipate that folks will become so accustomed to working, learning, shopping, and interacting at home that they won't want to leave that "cocoon" to worship with Christ's body.

I don't share this view. In fact, I see the threat of isolation as a tremendous opportunity for real community. I suspect that the increased isolation that could afflict Internet surfers will *magnify* the need and desire for real, physical, human community. God created humans with an innate need for social inter-action and community. The Internet may offer a "vir-tual" community for work, study, and play; but the church offers actual community. Online Bible studies, chat rooms, and the like can be wonderful supple-ments to what the church offers, but nothing can replace the experience of Christ's body gathered for corporate worship.

The Internet is a *tool*, entrusted by God to the church to use wisely. If we are good stew-ards of this resource, it can complement and enhance the proclamation of the gospel and the work of the Kingdom. But like the printing press, the radio, and television, the Internet is *only* a tool. And in time there will be other tools.

I am certain of one thing: The media we use will change, but the truth of the gospel will remain the same. Praise be to God!

# *More Cool Places to Go*

The following are more United Methodist-related sites that you might find helpful and interesting. The general church agency and national level sites are perhaps helpful mostly for reference purposes. The local church sites provide useful information about ministry, as well as excellent clues to good web design. The rest of the sites contain resources that may offer insight and suggestions for ministry.

### General Church Agency Sites

*The General Commission on Archives and History.* Houses archives of resources regarding the history of The United Methodist Church.
*Location: **http://www.gcah.org***

*General Commission on Christian Unity and Interreligious Concerns (GCCUIC).* Includes links to local, regional, and global councils.
*Location: **http://www.umc.org/gccuic/index.htm***

*General Commission on United Methodist Men (UMM).* Explains the work of UMM. Includes links to special events for UMM, Scouting, prayer resources for men, and the "Moving United Methodists" service.
*Location: **http://www.ummen.org***

*General Council on Finance and Administration (GCFA).* Explains the work of GCFA, lists current GCFA events, and includes *GCFA News*, the agency's newsletter.
*Location: **http://www.gcfa.org***

### Other National Level Sites

*United Methodist Communications.* The frame-enhanced page includes links to United Methodist News Service, EcuFilm, media services, the General Council on Ministries Calendar of Meetings, *Interpreter* magazine, and more.
*Location: **http://www.umc.org/umcom***

*United Methodist Publishing House.* Includes online versions of *Circuit Rider* and *Newscope.* Contains information about *Disciple* Bible study, including how to register for training events.
*Location: **http://www.umph.org/index.html***

*Cokesbury Online.* Contains a bookstore for Abingdon Press products, access to ordering online versions of *Faithlink, LinC,* and *FaithNow,* and a searchable database of Cokesbury bookstores nationwide.
*Location: **http://www.cokesbury.org/col/index.html***

*National Youth Ministry Organization (NYMO).* Contains links to NYMO Steering Committee, Youth Service Fund, service projects, and other youth-related sites.
*Location: **http://www.umc.org/nymo***

*United Methodist-Related Chaplains and Campus Ministers.* Includes e-mail addresses and a partial list of the more than 700 campus ministries supported by United Methodists.
*Location: **http://www.gbhem.org/gbhem/cmlist.html***

*The United Methodist Church Civic Youth Serving Agencies/Scouting Home Page.* Supports the connection between United Methodism and the Boy Scouts, Girl Scouts, and Camp-Fire Boys and Girls.
*Location: **http://www.umcscouting.org***

*Religion Mega-Site.* Developed by Aphids Communications, this site contains links to religious resources and an icon and image archive, as well as help for creating and housing a church home page.
*Location: **http://www.aphids.com/megasite***

### Local Church Level Sites
*Hibben United Methodist Church, Mount Pleasant, South Carolina.* This award winner offers a good balance of attractive layout, information, and speedy download.
*Location: **http://www.gbgm-umc.org/churches/hibben***

*Mount Oak United Methodist Church, Mitchellville, Maryland*. This well-designed web page includes pull-down menus to save space, RealAudio sermons, and several built-in search engines.
*Location: http://www.mtoak.org*

### Resources for Ministry

*United Methodist Church Doctrine*. Contains excerpts from "Our Doctrinal Heritage" and "Our Doctrinal History" found in *The Book of Discipline of The United Methodist Church*.
*Location:*
*http://www.netins.net/showcase/umsource/umdoct.html*

*Methodist Archives and Research Centre*. Contains online exhibitions of John Wesley and his preachers, women in Methodism, as well as a manuscript and picture gallery of Methodist archival material.
*Location:*
*http://rylibweb.man.ac.uk/data1/dg/text/method.html*

*Wesley Fellowship Groups*. Contains the participant's guide for Wesley Fellowship Groups training program. Originally written by Rev. G. Rowan Rogers of South Africa, with significant revisions.
*Location: http://www.easum.com/others/wfgp.htm*

*Internet Church Directory*. Contains links to web sites of United Methodist churches in Asia, Africa, and Europe.
*Location: http://www.umc.org/churches/internat.html*

*Africa University Home Page*. Explains the university's mission and work, and contains news and a photo gallery.
*Location: http://www.umc.org/benevol/africa/index.html*

*Sermons From Duke Chapel*. Contains full-text sermons delivered in the chapel of the United Methodist-related Duke University, Durham, North Carolina.
*Location:*
*http://www.chapel.duke.edu/sermons/default.htm*

96